EMBROIDERIES
FROM AN
ENGLISH GARDEN

The four seasons in surface embroidery. Outline p. 107.
Designed by the author, embroidered by Pat Harvey.

Embroideries from an English Garden

Projects and techniques
in surface embroidery

CAROL ANDREWS

RUTH BEAN

First published in 1997 by Ruth Bean Publishers,
an imprint of The Crowood Press Ltd, Ramsbury,
Marlborough, Wiltshire SN8 2HR

www.crowood.com

This impression 2014

British Library Cataloguing-in-Publication Data
A catalogue record for this book is available from the British Library.

ISBN 978 0 903585 34 7

Embroidery editor: Leila Ridell
Design: Alan Bultitude
Photo styling: Caryl Mossop
Photography: Mark Scudder & Les Goodey, Photographic Dept, Cambridge University Library

Fig.1, p.68 reprinted by permission of Reed Consumer Books from *Creative Needlecraft* by Lynette De Denne, published by Octopus.

Cover: *Late Summer in the garden*. Designed and worked by the author in stranded cottons, metallic thread, beads and padding, on fine weave linen. Embroidery actual size.
   The linen was hand-dyed by Chris Dobson using fibre reactive (Procion H-E) dyes, dissolved to the manufacturer's instructions (*see* Suppliers, p.112). For every 3 grams of fabric the formula is: gold 3.5 ml, brown 0.2 ml, red 0.2 ml.

Printed and bound in China by CTPS

Contents

Embroideries & colour illustrations

Carol Andrews – *The garden in Summer*, cover; *Red hellebore*, 19; *Lilac*, 33; *Autumn*, 49;
    Autumn bouquet, 56; *Clover*, 76; *Forget-me-not*, 81; *Bluebells*, 85; *Daffodils*, 92; *Apples*, 97.
June Batchelor – *Viola*, 28; *Two pansies*, 30, 31.
Elsie Anna Burton – *Spring*, 23; *Summer*, 37; *Honeysuckle*, 41; *Sampler*, 65.
Barbara Cockerham – *Winter*, 11; *Christmas*, 60. • Moira Postans – *Poppies*, 91.
Pat Harvey – *Four seasons*, frontispiece; *Winter jasmine & heather*, 14; *Two posies*, 17.
Doris Ward – *Butterfly*, 44; *Blackberries*, 53. • Drawing for *Summer*, 6. • Wallpaper adapted for *Posies*, 15.

The author's drawing for 'Summer', p. 37.
Water-colour pencils on paper.

Introduction

In many ways I am a typical teacher. I want to tell others about the excitement and satisfaction to be found in embroidery and I enjoy showing them new methods and techniques.

This book is about a highly individual type of embroidery, developed over the years, and it began life as a teaching aid. I used to teach a different type of embroidery each year, but once we discovered how to interpret flowers in surface and raised embroidery my students wanted nothing else.

My designs, like the drawing opposite, were taken from the garden and were tested in class, week by week. We explored many possibilities, using traditional stitches with different threads, fabrics, padding and beads and gradually a distinctive style began to emerge, like a rare butterfly coming out of its chrysalis.

The garden which inspired the designs has a certain claim to fame. My house at Olton in the West Midlands was once the home of Edith Holden. Her diary for the year 1906, illustrated with her own paintings from nature, became a best-seller in the 1970s as *The Country Diary of An Edwardian Lady*. Among the entries she mentions the birds and plants in her garden.

I wanted to paint in thread all the plants of my garden; the flowers, fruits, berries and hips that delight me season by season, and to capture permanently their passing beauty.

As well as embroidery I teach botanical painting, and my art and embroidery students work together, understanding the same concepts and terminology. The embroiderers portray flowers with the same delicate touch as the painters: both create three-dimensional forms on a two-dimensional surface, and use shading to achieve it.

Shadow and the illusion of depth are created by combining light, mid and dark toned threads, as can be seen in the embroideries themselves.

Despite the fact that the designs are all drawn in the same hand, each embroiderer will interpret them in a slightly different way so, unlike cross stitch, each embroidery is unique. As you get used to the techniques and stitches, you will increasingly find you can interpret a design in your own way.

I hope that the enthusiasm and dedication of my students, which has achieved such impressive results and inspired me, will be passed on through this book and produce many more converts to the pleasures of surface embroidery.

Happy stitching!

Acknowledgements

I am indebted to all the people whose special contributions have made this book possible.

Firstly I would like to thank my friends and students who have patiently and enthusiastically stitched their way through so many designs, and to acknowledge those who have contributed embroideries to the book: June Batchelor, Elsie Anna Burton, Barbara Cockerham, Pat Harvey, Moira Postans and Doris Ward. Special thanks go to my botanical painting teacher Anne-Marie Evans whose tips and techniques I have adapted for embroidery.

I am grateful to Leila Riddell for her technical review of the text and valuable suggestions; to Caryl Mossop for her inspired presentation of the embroideries; to Mark Scudder and Les Goodey for their fine photography. My particular thanks go to Nigel Bean for his careful editing and to Ruth Bean for her encouragement and guidance throughout.

How to use the book

The projects are grouped by season. Within each season you will find simpler as well as more complex designs. You can also extract a section from a larger design to make an individual project: see *Tips & suggestions*, p. 68. Embroideries are shown actual size or reduced when space requires it.

Before starting you should read carefully the section *In preparation*, p. 66.

- *Prepare the materials* you need: measurements are given in both inches and centimetres.

- *Prepare threads* by combining those you already have with those listed in the project table. Compare them with the illustration of the finished embroidery and take the list with you if you plan to buy threads.

- For ease of comparison *the tables*, showing threads, stitches and effects, are placed as near as possible to the illustrations. They also show the order of working. The thread numbers shown are those used in the embroideries illustrated. Single threads are used unless stated otherwise.

- The *pattern outlines* at the end of the book are actual size. Copy them and follow instructions on p. 67 for transferring them to the fabric.

- *Embroidery notes*, like the tables, are set out in the order of working. Stitches and effects shown in **bold** type are explained in detail in the **Stitches & Techniques** section. When there is a choice of shade, thread numbers are quoted in the text.

- *Working diagrams* are included throughout to explain specific steps. The diagrams are not intended to reflect the number of stitches in the actual embroidery.

- *Padding diagrams* are also included. Those which are shown actual size are described as 'padding outline' in the caption. Copy and use them as templates to cut out the padding material. Others, either reduced or enlarged, serve only as guides and are described in the caption as 'padding guide'. For these, copy and use the corresponding section of the pattern outline as a template. See also *Padding*, p. 95. Vilene padding requires a single layer unless otherwise stated.

- *Guide lines* for the direction of stitches are provided, either on the working diagram or the pattern outline. Petals and leaves are normally worked from edge to centre. For leaves use the side veins to angle long & short stitch.

- *A word on shading:* as light is cast from the upper left in most of the designs, petals, leaves, berries and even stems are generally light on the left, becoming darker towards the right.

- The working diagrams in **Stitches & Techniques** show the needle going up and down through the fabric, in contrast with the horizontal movement used for sewing. This is important for achieving clear and well defined stitches.

The finished projects

You may want to consider in advance what you will do with the finished work. Some embroiderers enjoy the stitching itself so much that the finished piece is simply added to their collection, possibly to be handed down as an heirloom. Some may mount an exhibition. Others may plan their work as a special gift.

The larger projects tend to be framed and used as pictures which several generations can enjoy. The smaller projects find more varied uses, including wedding presents, domestic decorations and cards.

The projects

The garden through the seasons

Winter

Designed by the author, embroidered by Barbara Cockerham

The beauty of my garden, which formerly belonged to Edith Holden, is more subtle in winter than at any other time of the year. Simpler forms and shapes, often overlooked in more colourful and flamboyant seasons, are more easily appreciated at this time.

An unusual golden-hued ivy covers the wall beside the front door, glowing with yellows and greens against the mellow brown of the brickwork. Elsewhere, bright red cotoneaster berries mingle with the yellow flowers of winter jasmine, and the hedge of clipped holly. All these plants, together with sprigs of yew in flower, appear in this design for 'Winter'. Embroidery reduced size.

You will need

Embroidery hoop, 10 in (25 cm). Closely woven linen or satinised cotton, 14 in (35 cm) square. Ecru or pearl, gold and black seed beads. Vilene padding. Threads: DMC stranded cotton.

Embroidery	Colour	Thread No
Ivy leaves	yellow-green	472, 471, 470, 469, 937
stems	khaki-brown	613, 612, 611, 610
Yew stems, leaves	green	369, 368, 320, 367, 319
flowers	ecru	ecru
Cotoneaster stems & leaves	green, khaki-brown	*471, 470, 611*
berries	pink, red, black, white	761, 760, 3328, 347, 310, blanc neige
Holly berries	pink, red, white	754, 351, 817, *blanc neige*
leaves	grey-green, ecru	524, 523, 522, 520, *ecru*
Jasmine flowers	yellow, green, ecru	445, 307, *471, 470, ecru*
stems	green	*472, 471, 470*
Rose hips	red, green, gold, white	*351*, 350, 349, 3347, 725, 783, *blanc neige*

The embroidery sections and threads are listed in order of working. Repeat threads are shown in **bold italics**.

Embroidery notes

Transfer the outline and mount the fabric, see pp. 67, 103. Stitches and effects are listed with each part. They are highlighted in the instructions in **bold** type and explained in detail under *Stitches & Techniques*.

Use the finished embroidery as a guide to shading. The project is worked clockwise, starting from the top. Use single strands of thread throughout unless stated otherwise.

2. Pad the four largest leaves with a layer of vilene, cutting out the central vein as shown in FIG 1.

3. Where one leaf overlaps another, leave a small gap between the **padding** of the two leaves, cut from the padding of the lower leaf. The cut **padded** shapes should fit just inside the **split** stitch outlines.

4. Lay the shapes on your fabric and check the fit, trimming where necessary.

GOLDEN IVY

Stitches & effects

Split stitch, padding with overcast stitch, long & short stitch, satin stitch, straight stitch, stem stitch.

1. Work the outlines of all the leaves in **split** stitch in a mid green thread, e.g. 471.

1. Ivy leaf
Guide to padding, with side veins. The tapering gap indicates the central vein. Mark the side veins on the padding with a transfer pencil to help angle the stitches.

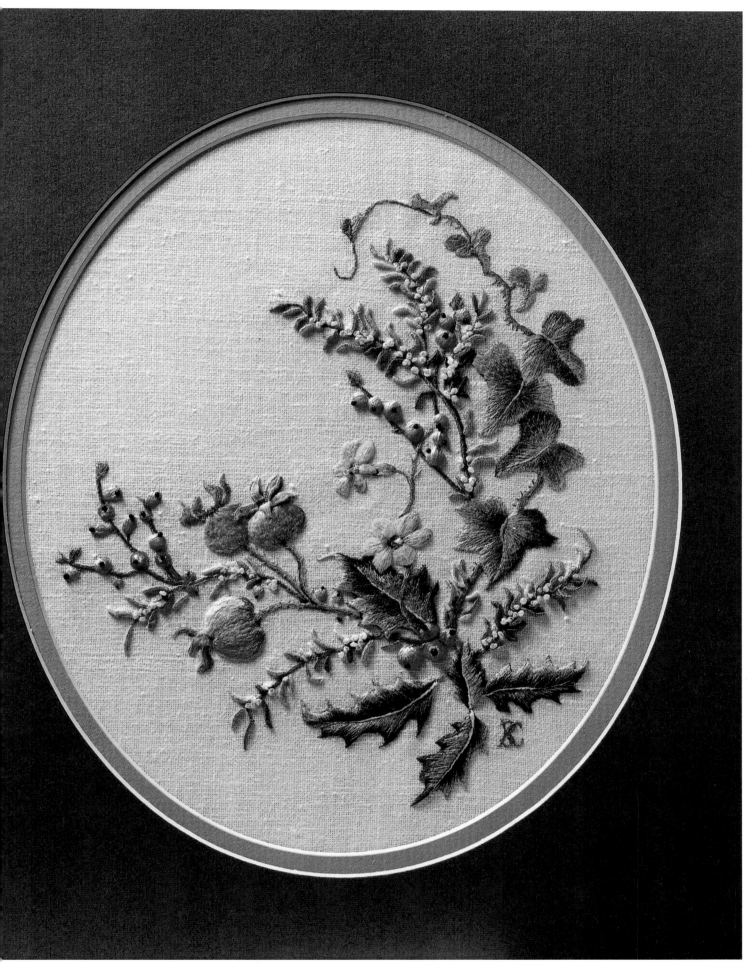

5. Apply the **padding** to the fabric with overcast stitches.

6. Mark the side veins on the padding with a transfer pencil to show the direction of the stitches, FIG 1.

7. Work all the leaves except the two smallest ones in **long & short** stitch. Reduce the numbers of stitches on second and subsequent rows to fit the narrowing space.

8. **Satin** stitch or **split** stitch can be used to fill the smallest leaves. Work the stems in **stem** stitch, placing the darker tones mostly on the right.

9. Work the central veins of the ivy leaves in **stem** stitch using yellow green (472).

10. Apply small **straight** stitches at right angles to the stem, representing the suckers which hold the ivy to the wall.

 YEW SPRIGS See also *Christmas*, p. 60.
Stitches & effects
Bullion knots, couching, French knots, stem stitch, beading.

1. Using two strands of a green from the list for yew leaves, work a leaf with a **bullion knot**. Don't mix different shades in the same knot.

2. To form a curved leaf anchor the **bullion knot** with a single **couching** stitch.

3. Work the other yew leaves in the same way, selecting threads from the greens listed to provide variety.

4. Embroider the stem in closely worked rows of **stem** stitch.

5. Form the pale wintry flowers as clusters of **French knots** worked with three strands of ecru. Seed **beads** may be used as well as, or instead of, **French knots**.

COTONEASTER BERRIES
See also *Christmas*, p. 60
Stitches & effects

Stem stitch, split stitch, long & short stitch, satin stitch, French knots, beading.

1. Work the stems in **stem** stitch and the small leaves in **satin** stitch.

2. Outline the edges of the berries in **split** stitch using red (3328). Make the stitches quite small and ease each previous stitch back onto the outline with the subsequent stitch. The outline must curve and not look jagged.

3. The berries in the embroidery include highlights. Work some of them in **long & short** stitch, some in **satin** stitch, and some in rings of **split** stitch.

4. Form the dark tip of each of the smaller berries with a **French knot** worked with two strands of black (310). For the larger berries use a small black seed **bead**.

HOLLY LEAVES & BERRIES
See *Christmas*, p. 60
Stitches & effects

Split stitch, padding, long & short stitch, stem stitch.

1. Work the outlines of the leaves in a mid green (523), and of the berries in red (351), all in **split** stitch.

2. Ease the stitches round the berries to form a curved outline, as for the cotoneaster berries.

3. **Pad** the four lowest leaves with a layer of vilene, leaving a tapering gap along the central vein, as for the golden ivy.

4. **Pad** *only* the lower half of the top holly leaf since the jasmine overlaps its upper section. See FIG 2.

2. Holly leaf. Guide to padding lower half of top leaf

5. Work the leaves in **long & short** stitch.

6. Work the central veins in **stem** stitch using ecru.

7. **Pad** all four berries with 2 layers of vilene, as shown in FIG 3.

8. Apply an initial layer of **padding** to the centres.

9. Apply a second layer of padding on top of the first, as shown in FIG 3.

3. Holly berries. Guide to padding
Left: first layer of padding. The broken lines show the outlines of the berries. The solid lines show the first layers of padding, in the centre.
Right: second layer of padding. Leave a narrow gap in the padding between the berries, shown shaded.

WINTER JASMINE
See p. 14 and *Christmas,* p. 60
Stitches & effects

Stem stitch, split stitch, padding, long & short stitch, straight stitch, beading, detached chain stitch.

1. Work the stems in **stem** stitch, shading from light on the left to dark on the right. Use a single strand in three different tones of green.
2. Outline the flowers in **split** stitch in yellow (445) and **pad** each petal with a layer of vilene.
3. Work the petals and calyx in **long & short** stitch.
4. Work the centre of the flowers in short **straight** stitches. Outline the centres with a dark crescent shape in **split** stitch, to create a shadow.
5. Use a single seed **bead** for the stigma of each flower.
6. Work the sepals of the upper flower in **detached chain** stitch in green (471).

ROSE HIPS
Stitches & effects

Split stitch, padding, long & short stitch, embroidered picots, stem stitch, straight stitch.

1. The outline shapes in FIG 4 represent the two top hips, designated *hips 1 & 2.* The single lower hip is a little larger and referred to as *hip 3.*
2. Start with *hips 1 & 2:* the outlines are indicated by broken lines. Work the outlines, apart from areas where the sepals overlap the hips, in **split** stitch using gold (783). Make sure the edges are nicely rounded.

3. Prepare the two different layers of **padding** for *hips 1, 2 & 3.* The first layer is smaller. *Hip 3* uses the same **padding** as *hip 2,* but enlarged a little.
4. Apply the first layer of **padding,** shaped to fit the centres, as shown in FIG 4a.
5. Apply the second layer of **padding,** which must be cut to fit just inside the **split** stitch outlines of the hips, as shown in FIG 4b. Allow for the bulge created by the first layer.

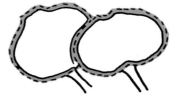

4. Rose hips
Guide to padding, hips 1 & 2.
a. The solid lines show the first layer of padding. Adapt hip 2 outline for hip 3.

b. The solid lines show the second layer. Adapt the hip 2 outline for hip 3.

Leave a narrow gap in the padding of the overlapped hip.

6. Draw the directional guide lines onto the padding with a transfer pencil, see FIG 5.
7. Work *hips 1 & 2* in **long & short** stitch.
8. Use adjacent rows of **split** or **stem** stitch to work *hip 3.*

5. Rose hips
Guide lines for angling of stitches.
Mark the lines on the padding. Adapt hip 2 guide lines for hip 3.

9. The sepals, shown in FIG 6, are basically triangular, making them perfect subjects for **embroidered picots.** Work all the sepals of *hip 2* in this way, as well as the central sepal of *hip 3.*

6. Rose hips. Position of embroidered picots on hip 2.

10. Work the stems in **stem** stitch. Use short **straight** stitches to represent the small thorns along the stem.

Many of the embroiderers who contributed to the book started with this design. Actual size.

Winter jasmine & heather

Designed by the author,
embroidered by Pat Harvey

Embroidery notes

1. Transfer the outline and mount the fabric, see pp. 67, 106. *Don't* transfer the V-shaped leaves of the heather, which will be added naturally as work progresses. Stitches and effects highlighted in the instructions in **bold** type are explained in detail under *Stitches & Techniques*.

2. *Heather.* Work the stems in **open fishbone** stitch, the flowers in **detached chain** stitch and the buds in **French knots**.

3. *Jasmine.* Outline the flower petals in **split** stitch and fill with **satin** stitch *over* the outline. Apply a few small **straight** stitches to the flower centres for a shadow effect.

4. Work the stamens in **stem** stitch with green-gold and apply a single gold seed **bead** to each for the stigma.

5. Work the stems in **stem** stitch, and the sepals of the bud and the small leaves along the stem in **detached chain** stitch, using green (280). Work the sepals of the upper right flower in **satin** stitch, using green-gold (279). Work the jasmine bud in yellow **satin** stitch (295) on top of the heather **fishbone** stitch.

You will need

Embroidery hoop, 6 in (15 cm). Closely woven linen or satinised cotton, 10 in (25 cm) square. Gold seed beads. Threads: Anchor stranded cotton.

Embroidery	Colour	Thread No	Stitches & effects
Heather stems	olive-green	281	open fishbone stitch
flowers	mauve	96, 97	detached chain stitch
buds	mauve	**96, 97**	French knots
Jasmine flower petals	yellow	292, 295	split, satin stitch
flower centres	rust brown, green	309, 280	straight stitch
stamen	green-gold	279	stem stitch
stigma	gold		beading
stem	green-gold	**279**	stem stitch
sepals, leaf buds	green-gold, green	**279, 280**	detached chain, satin stitch

The embroidery sections and threads are listed in order of working. Repeat threads are shown in ***bold italics***.

Two posies

Designs adapted by the author from a fragment of old wallpaper, embroidered by Pat Harvey as framed lids for porcelain jars. Shown actual size.

During the winter months, when the garden requires less attention, much of our spare time is given over to decorating the house. We have spent many hours stripping, restoring and redecorating the top floor room Edith Holden used as a bedroom. In a recess, behind some bookshelves fixed to the wall, we found several layers of old wallpaper. On the bottom layer were fragments of a floral paper that must have been very familiar to her, and the small bouquet on this paper inspired my 'Posy' design.

The flower petals on the wallpaper are quite vague, so some imagination was used to translate the design. The smaller outline is drawn to the same scale as the wallpaper design, and was worked on fine cream Irish linen, using one strand of embroidery cotton. If you prefer a larger scale use the enlarged outline and two strands of cotton. Either posy is suitable for less experienced embroiderers.

The turn of the century wallpaper which inspired the posies. Actual size.

You will need

Embroidery hoop, 4 in (10 cm). Closely woven cream linen, 8 in (20 cm) square.
Threads: DMC stranded cotton.

Embroidery	Colour	Thread No	Stitches & effects
Flower petals	pink, magenta, mauve, purple, blue	3689, 3731, 600, 554, 552, 341, 340	split stitch, seeding stitch padding, satin stitch
Flower centres	blue, purple	*341, 552*	satin stitch
Leaves	grey-green, green	522, 520, 368	close fishbone stitch, straight stitch, satin stitch
Flower buds	blue, purple, pink	*341, 552, 3689, 3731*	split stitch, seeding stitch padding, satin stitch
Sepals	grey-green	*522*	detached chain stitch, straight stitch
Stems	grey-green, green	*522, 520, 368*	stem stitch
Decorative dots	wine red	315	French knots

The embroidery sections and threads are listed in order of working. Repeat threads are shown in **bold italics**.

Embroidery notes - round frame

Use single strands of thread throughout except for French knots which need two strands.

These notes can also be used for the modified *Posy* in the **oval** frame. There are, however, some colour variations in this version.

1. Transfer the outline and mount the fabric, see pp. 67, 105. Draw in the guide lines showing the angle of stitching with a transfer pencil, or follow the colour drawing on p. 17. Stitches and surface effects highlighted in the instructions in **bold** type are explained in detail under *Stitches & Techniques.*

Flower petals

2. Start by outlining the outer petal edges only of the central blue flower in **split** stitch, in pale blue (341): don't work the lines which join petals, FIGS 1 & 2. Make the stitches quite small and ease each previous stitch back onto the outline with the subsequent stitch. The outline must curve and not look jagged.

3. At the pointed end of a petal or leaf, end one line of **split** stitch and begin a new one, working an initial **straight** stitch back into the point and continuing the outline in **split** stitch. This outline, will form a firm edge to work over in **satin** stitch. Repeat *Notes 2. & 3.* for the other flowers and leaves, in the matching colours.

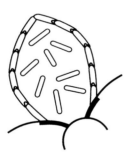

1. Enlarged petal shape

Work the split stitch outline, but not the lines (shown thicker) between petals, before adding seeding stitches in the centre for light padding.

4. Before proceeding in **satin** stitch work a few **seeding** stitches in the centre of each petal to provide light **padding**, see FIG 1. This padding is not required for the curved red petals flanking two pink flowers at the top and lower right, nor for leaves.

5. Work the petals in **satin** stitch, making sure you completely cover the outline and padding. Follow FIG 2, which also shows how to keep the stitches at an even angle.

Flower centres

6. Work the centre of each open flower in **satin** stitch. Don't outline or pad this area. Use blue (340) for the left hand flower and purple (552) for the right.

Leaves & buds

7. Work the larger leaves in **satin** stitch. Note how veining has been added with **straight** stitches in a contrasting green on some leaves. Work the smaller leaves in either **close fishbone** or **satin** stitch.

8. Outline the flower bud edges, using small **split** stitches and easing each previous stitch back onto the curved outline. Use **seeding** stitch padding, as for the petals, and complete in **satin** stitch.

Stems & dots

9. Finish off by working the stems in **stem** stitch, the sepals in **detached chain** stitch, and the dots in **French knots**.

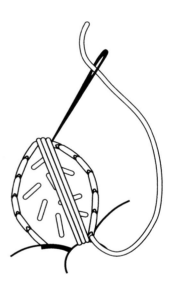

2. Working a leaf or petal in satin stitch

Work the satin stitches to completely cover the outlining split stitches and the seeding stitches. To maintain the stitches at a constant angle, start from the centre and work to one side, then, taking the needle through the back of the stitches, return to the centre and work the other half.

Two posies

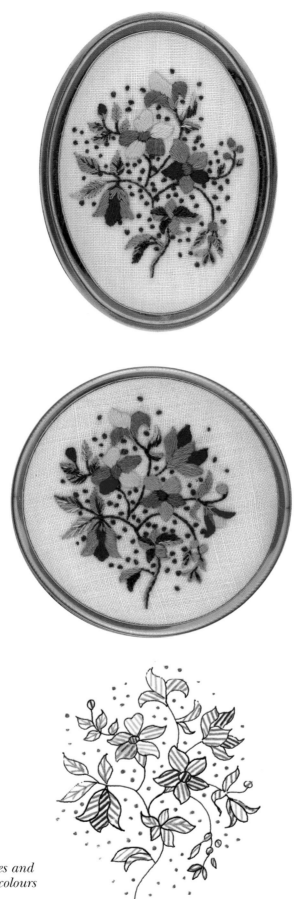

Round posy
Direction of satin stitches and guide to shading, with colours matching the threads.

Red hellebore

Designed and embroidered by the author

Hellebores seem able to defy the severest of English wintry weather. They start to bloom in February and the flowers frequently linger on until April or May.

*The red hellebore in this design, **helleboris orientalis**, was drawn to give plenty of practice in long & short stitch. It uses the subtle shades of Appleton crewel wools, with highlights in Madeira silk. DMC coton perlé was used for the French knots in the centre of the open flower.*

The embroidery illustrated was worked on a piece of early 20th century linen. Suitable alternatives are cotton twill fabric or a cotton/linen mixture, not too closely woven. Evenweave linen is not suitable as it is woven too openly. Embroidery reduced size.

You will need

Embroidery hoop, 8 in (20 cm). Cotton twill or linen union, 12 in (30 cm) square.
Threads: Appleton crewel wool (A); Madeira silk (M); DMC coton perlé (D) size 5.

Embroidery	Colour	Thread No	Stitches & effects
Flower highlights	pink	M0503	split stitch, long & short stitch
Flowers and buds	dull rose pink	A144, 145, 149	split stitch, long & short stitch
Centre open flower	green, cream	D581, 746	French knots
	dull rose pink	*A149*	straight stitch
Leaf highlights	green	M1409	long & short stitch
Leaves	grass green	A251, 253, 254, 256	split stitch, long & short stitch
Stem	grass green	*A251, 253, 254, 256*	stem stitch

The embroidery sections and threads are listed in order of working. Repeat threads are shown in ***bold italics***.

Embroidery notes

1. Transfer the outline and mount the fabric, see pp. 67, 21. Draw in the guide lines showing the angle of stitching with a transfer pencil.

When working in silk use 2 strands: for wool use only one. For French knots use 2 or 3 strands of coton perlé. Stitches and effects highlighted in the instructions in **bold** type are explained in detail under ***Stitches & Techniques***. Use the embroidery as a guide for shading.

The open flower

2. Outline the outer edges only of the open flower in **split** stitch with pink silk (0503). Don't work the lines between petals. Emphasise curves by easing each previous stitch back along the outline with the stitch being worked.

The outer petal edges are wider than the inner ones next to the stamen area. This provides an opportunity to practise working **long & short** stitch from a wide space into a narrow one.

3. Start with the lower right petal, working over the **split** stitch edging in **long & short** stitch. Use pink silk for the first (outer) row and rose pink wool for the following rows. Try to create an even tension on each stitch, particularly when working in silk. It helps to separate the two strands of silk *before* pairing them in the needle as this thread has quite a lot of twist in it, see *Threads* p. 66.

4. Graduate the shading from light at the edges to the darkest rose pink nearest the centre. Variations in light and shade are important for the natural appearance of a flower and must be followed.

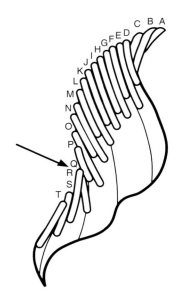

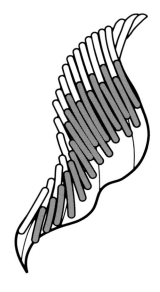

*1. Large bud of Hellebore –
starting the left hand petal*

The end of stitch A is covered by
B, and the ends of B & C by D.
Diagrams enlarged for clarity. You
may need more stitches than are
shown in Figs 1 to 3.

*2. Large bud of Hellebore –
continuing the left hand petal*

Adjusting stitches to the curved
edge. Stitch Q is pivoted on R and
stitch T is shown split into the side
of S. These techniques help adapt
the angles of stitches to the curve.

*3. Large bud of Hellebore –
working the second row*

Make sure that the 'brickwork'
effect is maintained across the
petal to create the soft, diffuse line
which is the essential feature of
this stitch.

When mixing stitches of pure silk with stitches in crewel wool, work the silk before the wool wherever possible as the threads will blend better.

Two of the *Hellebore* petals have silk highlights down both sides as well as on their outer edges, but the two rear petals are in shadow and have dark sides. The top petal has a highlight on the side which lies over its neighbour but none where it lies under the adjacent petal.

5. Form the centre of the flower by working **French knots** closely together in coton perlé. The number of threads used for the knots can be varied to add interest and texture. In this case the cream ones were worked in one or two strands, and the green ones from one strand on the left to three on the right. Work the central **French knot**

with two strands of dark rose pink wool (149), and from this work three small **straight** stitches with a single strand of the same thread.

The large bud

6. Outline the bud in split stitch using rose pink (144) wool. Work it in **long & short** stitch, starting with the left hand petal. Work the first row in pink silk (0503), FIGS 1 & 2.

For the correct angle of stitching you will need to cover the ends of some **long & short** stitches with following ones, like *A* to *C* in FIG 1. This will allow you to change angles subtly and smoothly.

Similarly, at the lower edge of the same petal, arrowed in FIG 2, the angle of stitching has to be adjusted by pivoting stitches, e.g. *R & Q*, at a

Pattern outline showing direction of stitches.

common needle hole to accommodate the curve. On such a curve it is impossible to work **long & short** stitch rigidly. Maintain your length of stitch and don't fall into the trap of making stitches shorter and shorter as you work down the edge.

Occasionally you will need to split into the sides, rather than the ends, of stitches for slight changes of angle, see stitches *T & S*, FIG 2. Maintain an interleaved, 'brickwork', effect for all rows and you won't go far wrong.

7. FIG 3 shows the second row of stitches in a darker tone. Complete the petal, darkening the tone with each successive row, and work the final row over the inner **split** stitched edge.

Complete the petals in **long and short** stitch. The techniques learned above will be useful for the right-hand petal.

Leaves, small bud & stems

8. Working in **split** stitch, outline the leaves in mid-tone green (253), and the smaller bud in pink silk (0503), to form a firm edge over which to work the **long & short** stitches.

9. With the exception of the stems, work the rest of the design in **long & short** stitch.

10. Work the stems in adjacent rows of **stem** stitch.

21

Spring

Designed by the author, embroidered by Elsie Anna Burton

One of the simple pleasures of spring is the sight of the peachy red japonica, flowering on the old outhouse wall beside the kitchen window. Blue tits, perhaps descendants of those painted by Edith Holden in her 1906 Diary, still frequent the garden, busily investigating the nest box lodged in the branches of the japonica. They are an amusing sight from the kitchen window.

*At the foot of the japonica (Pink lady) is a variegated creeping periwinkle, **Vinca major variegata**. Both plants appear in this design for 'Spring', together with rhododendron (Cynthia), berberis in flower, heather, viola, grape hyacinth, aubrietia and forget-me-nots. These plants are just a few of the many delights of the garden in springtime. Embroidery reduced size.*

You will need

Embroidery hoop, 10 in (25 cm). Closely woven linen or satinised cotton, 14 in (35 cm) square. Fine crewel needles. Seed beads: cream, yellow, blue, mauve. Vilene padding.
Threads: DMC stranded cotton; Madeira silk (M).

Embroidery	Colour	Thread No
Rhododendron leaves, stem	grey-green	504, 503, 502, 501, 500
petals, buds	pink, red	605, 604, 3806, 3805, 3803, 3802, 902
stamens, pistil	green, yellow	M1409, 0112
Berberis flowers	yellow, gold	725, 726, 783
stem	gold, brown	*783*, 781,
leaves	yellow-green	3348, 3347, 3346, 3345
Heather stems	green	*3348, 3346, 3345*
flowers	deep red	*3803*
Periwinkle flower	blue, mauve, yellow	341, 340, 3746, 333, 727
leaves	green, yellow	472, 471, 470, 469, *727*
stem	green, blue	*471, 470, 469*, 3746
Japonica flowers	peach-red, yellow	353-1, 3778, 355, *3802, 727*
leaves, stem	green, pink	*3348, 3347, 3346, 3778, 352*
Grape hyacinth	blue, mauve	*341, 340, 3746, 333*
leaf, stem	yellow-green	*3348, 3347, 3346*
Forget-me-not flower	blue, yellow	775, 3325, 3755, *726*
stem	green	*471*
Aubrietia flowers, stem	mauve, green	210, 209, 208, 327, *472*
Viola flower and centre	mauve, yellow	211, *210, 209, 208*, 550, 727
leaves and stem	yellow-green, gold	*471, 470, 469, 783*

The embroidery sections and threads are listed in order of working. Repeat threads are shown in ***bold italics***.

Embroidery notes

Transfer the outline and mount the fabric, see pp. 67, 104. Stitches and effects are listed with each part. They are highlighted in the instructions in **bold** type and explained in detail under *Stitches & Techniques*.

Use the finished embroidery as a guide to shading. The project is worked from the centre of the design outwards, using single strands of thread except for **French** and **bullion knots**.

RHODODENDRON

Stitches & effects

Split stitch, padding with overcast stitch, long & short, stem, straight, seeding, and satin stitch, bullion knots, couching, beading.

Outlining & padding

1. Work the outlines of all leaves, flowers and buds in **split** stitch, using a mid-tone thread of matching colour for each.

2. Use a single layer of vilene to **pad** all unshaded areas, see FIG 1.

1. Rhododendron, flower and leaves Guide to padding.

Outline all parts of the design in split stitch. Pad all unshaded areas. Allow for gaps in the padding between petals and along central veins of leaves, as shown by shading.

2. Rhododendron, flower and leaves Guide to working long & short stitches.

Transfer the directional lines onto the padding to angle the stitches.

Gaps are left in the **padding** where petals overlap leaves or other petals, and along the central veins of leaves.

3. Secure the **padding** with overcast stitches.

Petals & leaves

4. Follow FIG 2 and mark the direction of stitching on the vilene with a transfer pencil. Work the leaves and petals from edge to centre in **long & short** stitch. Work the central leaf veins and the bud **stem** in stem stitch.

5. Use a few small **straight** stitches in a dark thread (902) to define the dark streaks in the upper left petal; 3-strand for the upper part and 4-strand for the lower.

Flower centre, FIG 3

6. Work the outline of the crescent on the right in pale pink (605) **split** stitch. Pad this area in **seeding** stitch. Then work over it and over the outline in **satin** stitch (605) at the angles shown. Use the pivoting technique shown in FIG 3b to adjust the angle at intervals round the crescent. To do this enter the inner ends of two adjacent stitches through the same hole.

7. Working in from the edge, fill the centre with concentric rows of **split** stitch in dark red (3802). Add 3 long pale green **bullion knots** in single-stranded silk (M1409) for the stamens, and another in 2 strands of yellow silk (M0112). Anchor the **bullion knots** with occasional **couching** stitches to form slight curves. Tip the stamens with cream seed **beads** – the longest with a pale yellow one.

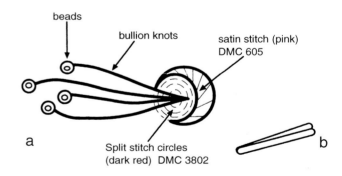

3. Rhododendron, flower centre

a. Work across the outline of the crescent-shaped area in satin stitch. Adjust the angle round the curve at intervals by pivoting threads as shown in b. Fill the circle on the left of the crescent with adjacent rings of split stitch. Add the stamens in silk bullion knots tipped with seed beads.

b. Pivoted threads, with the shared needle hole on the left.

BERBERIS (BARBERRY)

Stitches & effects

Split stitch, padding, long & short stitch, French knots, beading, bullion knots, couching stitch.

1. Outline all berberis leaves in **split** stitch in a mid-tone green 3347.

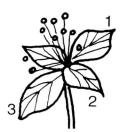

4. Berberis. Guide to padding and stitching

Pad leaves 1, 2 & 3. The directional lines show the angle of the long & short stitch.

2. Carefully **pad** leaves 1, 2 & 3 of the top group of flowers (FIG 4), and the lowest right leaf of the bottom group. Leave a small gap along the central veins of all 4 leaves.

3. Work the stem in **stem** stitch in gold and brown (783, 781).

4. Work the leaves in **long & short** stitch following the angles shown in FIG 4, and using **stem** stitch to define the central veins (3348, 3345).

5. Work yellow **French knots** and add yellow seed **beads** for the two upper groups of flowers.

6. Work the lowest berberis flowers, which are **bullion knot roses** made from small triangles of **bullion knots**. Follow FIG 5 and work each flower in two strands of yellow. You may find it easier to work this stitch in silk thread.

a   b   c

5. Larger berberis flower worked as a bullion knot rose

a. First work a triangle of bullion knots at the centre.

b. Add a ring of bullion knots, anchoring each with a couching stitch. The stitches are shown displaced outwards for greater clarity. The outer stitches can be left without couching to overlap the inner stitches.

c. Complete the centre with a single French knot made in several strands of thread or with a single bead.

HEATHER

Stitches

Open fishbone stitch, straight stitch, detached chain stitch.

Open fishbone stitch is excellent for representing heather leaves and the stem, which appear in two parts of the design.

1. Work the stems in **open fishbone** stitch (3346, 3345). **Straight** stitches may be added in 3348 to thicken the effect (see *Summer*, FIG 5). Make the stitches at the tips of the stems slightly smaller.

2. Work the flowers in **detached chain** stitch.

PERIWINKLE

Stitches & effects

Split stitch, padding, long & short stitch, stem stitch.

1. Outline the edges of the flower and leaves in **split** stitch, in matching colours, e.g. mauve 340, green 471.

2. Pad each petal with a single layer of vilene, leaving gaps between the petals. **Pad** the four largest leaves also, leaving the usual tapering gap for the central vein. FIG 6 shows the padding of the twisted leaf. Leave the shaded areas *without* **padding**.

6. Periwinkle. Padding outline for the twisted leaf

Pad only the unshaded areas. Shading indicates gaps in the padding.

3. Work the flower and leaves in **long & short** stitch.

Note the addition of a few stitches of blue into the leaves to harmonise with the flower.

4. Work the stem in **stem** stitch, using darker greens (469, 470, 471) and a little blue (3746).

JAPONICA

Stitches & effects

Split stitch, padding, alternative padding, couching, long & short stitch, satin stitch, fly stitch, straight stitch, beading, French knots, stem stitch.

7. Japonica Padding outline. Cut out unshaded shapes only, and apply one by one.

To pad narrow areas round petals, an alternative is to couch a thick thread. Work unshaded areas in long & short stitch, except for sections 1-3 in satin stitch.

1. Work all outlines in **split** stitch using a mid-tone matching colour (352, 3347).

2. FIG 7 shows the areas for **padding**. Cut and stitch the padding one piece at a time.

An alternative **padding** for the narrow areas round some petals is to raise the area by **couching** a thick thread, e.g. DMC soft embroidery thread.

3. Ensure all **padding** lies within the edges outlined in **split** stitch.

Petals

4. Work in **long & short** stitch, graduating from light to dark. Create the shadows in the centre with a few stitches of dark red (3802). Next work sections *1, 2 & 3* in **satin** stitch (355).

5. Green sepals are visible between the gaps in the petals. Work their outer edges in pale green (3348) **fly** stitch and fill them with one or two **straight** stitches in a darker green (3347).

6. Work **French knots** and add seed **beads**, both in cream, for the stamens.

Leaves

7. Shade the leaves from light to dark in **long & short** stitch, following the angles on the embroidery. Peach (352) highlights are added to the two younger leaves.

8. Work the stem in adjacent rows of **stem** stitch, shading from lighter on the left to darker on the right.

GRAPE HYACINTH

Stitches & effects

French knots, beading, split stitch, satin stitch, close fishbone stitch.

1. Starting from the top, work the flower in **French knots** in blues and mauves, remembering that the light is from the left, so the tone darkens towards the right and the lower edge. See FIG 8. Leave spaces to add seed **beads** between knots.

2. Work the outer edges and central vein of the leaf in **split** stitch using a mid-tone green (3347).

3. Work each side of the leaf in either **close fishbone** or **satin** stitch.

Note that at the twist in the leaf there is a sudden change from light to dark, as well as in the angle of the stitches. Much of the lower area of the leaf lies behind other plants, so is darker.

4. Work the stem in **stem** stitch using the yellow-greens listed.

8. Grape hyacinth. Guide to shading and angling of stitches
Use darker shades on the right side of the flower and the lower leaf. Note the change in shading and angle of stitches at the twist in the leaf.

26

FORGET-ME-NOT

Stitches

French knots, fly stitch, straight stitch, stem stitch.

1. Embroider the buds at the tip of the stem in **French knots**, using 2 and 3 strands of blue (775, 3325).

2. Work the open flowers in **fly** stitch using a darker tone (3755), FIG 9.

***9.** Forget-me-not. Enlarged centre of the open flowers*
Work in fly stitch, with a French knot to form the centre.

3. Embroider a single **French knot** in the centre of each flower using 2 strands of yellow (726).

4. Fill the middle of each petal with 2 or 3 **straight** stitches in blue (775).

5. Work the stem in **stem** stitch in green (471).

AUBRIETIA

Stitches & effects

Split stitch, padding, long & short stitch, satin stitch, beading, detached chain stitch, stem stitch.

1. Work in **split** stitch round the outlines of the flowers, but not round the buds, with a mid-tone mauve (209) thread.

2. **Pad** the unshaded parts of the flowers, fitting it carefully within the **split** stitch outlines, FIG 10.

3. Work the flowers in **long & short** stitch (210, 209) and the shaded parts afterwards in **satin** and **stem** stitch (208, 327).

4. You can use small cream seed **beads** for the centres of the flowers.

5. The buds (shown on the transfer but not on the embroidery) are optional and can be added in **detached chain** stitch.

6. Work the stem in **stem** stitch.

***10.** Aubrietia. Guide to padding and stitching of flowers and buds.*
Outline in split stitch and pad all unshaded areas. Work the flowers in long & short stitch and the shaded areas in satin stitch. The buds are optional.

VIOLA – see also *Viola* overleaf

Stitches & effects

Split stitch, padding, long & short stitch, French knots, stem stitch.

1. Outline the flowers and leaves in single-stranded **split** stitch (209 for flowers, 471 for leaves).

2. **Pad** the flower and leaves with a single layer of vilene, but *not* the shaded areas, see FIG 11. Draw in the directional guide lines from FIG 12 with a transfer pencil.

***11.** Viola*
Guide to padding.
Use the outline on p. 104 and pad only the unshaded areas of the flower and leaves.

3. Work the flowers and leaves in **long & short** stitch following the angles shown in Fig 12.

4. Work the flower centre with a yellow 4-stranded **French knot**.

5. Work the stems in adjacent rows of **stem** stitch.

6. Add a few final stitches of gold in the leaves to reflect the warm colour of the japonica flower and berberis stem elsewhere in the embroidery.

***12.** Viola*
Guide to stitching.
Follow the lines on the flower and leaves to angle the stitches.

Viola

Designed by the author, embroidered by June Batchelor

This 'mini'-project has been extracted from 'Spring'. Its simplicity of design and outline make it a satisfying piece to embroider and an attractive present. Embroidery actual size.

You will need

Embroidery hoop, 6 in (15 cm). Closely woven linen, 10 in (25 cm) square. Vilene padding. Yellow seed bead. Threads: DMC stranded cotton.

Embroidery	Colour	Thread No	Stitches & effects
Flower petals	mauve	211, 210, 209, 208, 550	split stitch, padding, long & short stitch
Flower centre	yellow	727	satin stitch, French knot, beading
Leaves	yellow,	*727*	split stitch, padding, long & short stitch
	yellow-green	472, 471, 470, 469	
Central vein	yellow-green	*472*	stem stitch
Stem	yellow-green	*472, 471, 469*	stem stitch

The embroidery sections and threads are listed in order of working. Repeat threads are shown in ***bold italics***.

Embroidery notes

1. Transfer the outline and mount the fabric, see pp. 67, 104. Use single strands of thread except for the French knot. Stitches and effects highlighted in the instructions in **bold** type are explained in detail under ***Stitches & Techniques***.

2. Outline the flowers and leaves in single-stranded **split** stitch (209 for flowers, 471 for leaves).

3. Photocopy the outline and use FIG 11 from *Spring* as a guide to padding. **Pad** the flower and leaves with a single layer, but not the shaded areas. Draw in the directional guide lines from FIG 12 in *Spring* with a transfer pencil.

4. Work the flowers and leaves in **long & short** stitch.

5. Work the flower centre in **satin** stitch. Add a yellow 3 or 4-stranded **French knot**, or seed **bead**.

6. Work the stems in adjacent rows of **stem** stitch, using the finished embroidery as a guide for shading.

7. Add a few final stitches of mauve, here and there in the leaves and stems, to reflect the colour of the flower and add shadow.

Two pansies

Designed by the author, embroidered by June Batchelor

Pansies appeal to many embroiderers so here we have a choice of two. The yellow and mauve pansy was drawn from a larger version of the heartsease pansy and each of its complementary colours looks brighter than it would by itself.

The pink pansy was adapted from a water-colour pencil drawing, made while the plant was still in its pot. Once its portrait was complete it was transferred to the shady side of the garden where it still flourishes.

You will need

Embroidery hoop, 6 in (15 cm). Fine weave linen or cotton, 10 in (25 cm) square.
Threads: DMC stranded cotton; Madeira silk (M).

Embroidery notes

The working notes apply to both designs unless otherwise stated. Use single strands of thread throughout except for the **French knot** in the centre of the PINK PANSY. Stitches and effects highlighted in the instructions in **bold** type are explained in detail under *Stitches & Techniques*.

1. Transfer the outline and mount the fabric, see pp. 67, 109.

Outlining and padding

2. Outline the flowers and leaves in **split** stitch using mid-tone matching colours.

3. **Pad** the open pansy flowers using a single layer, see FIG 1 and p. 96.

4. **Pad** both buds in the YELLOW/MAUVE PANSY. Remember to leave gaps in the padding where one petal overlaps another.

Pad the large bud for the PINK PANSY, as shown in FIG 2, but *not* the little bud. Ignore the green sepals at this stage.

1. Padding outline for the open flowers.

Left: yellow/mauve pansy.
Right: pink pansy.

5. For leaves where the underside is visible, **pad** only the underside, shown unshaded in FIG 3. **Pad** the remaining large leaf for each pansy normally, leaving a tapering gap for the central vein.

2. Pink pansy Enlarged left bud.

Pad only unshaded areas.

3. Both pansies. Guide to padding the underside of a leaf.

Where the underside of a leaf is visible and shown unshaded, pad only it.

Yellow/mauve pansy, embroidered by June Batchelor. Shown slightly enlarged.

Embroidery	*Colours*	*Thread No*	*Stitches & effects*
Flower petals	mauve, yellow	554, 552, 550, 745, 743, 742	split stitch, padding, long & short, straight stitch
Open flower centre	yellow, green	*743*, 470	satin stitch,
Sepals	green	*470*	embroidered picots, satin stitch
Leaves, upper side	green	472, 471, 469	split stitch, padding, long & short, stem stitch
Leaves, underside	blue, green	504, 503, 501	long & short stitch
Stems	green	*472, 471, 469*	stem stitch

The embroidery sections and threads are listed in order of working. Repeat threads are shown in ***bold italics***.

Pink pansy, embroidered by June Batchelor. Shown reduced.

Embroidery	Colours	Thread No	Stitches & effects
Flower petals	pink	3609, 3608, 3607, 917, 915, M0613	split stitch, padding, long & short stitch
Open flower centre	green pink	*472, 469* *M0613*	French knot, seeding stitch, bullion knots
Sepals	green	*471, 469*	embroidered picots, satin stitch
Leaves, stems – as for YELLOW/MAUVE PANSY, plus			
Small leaves	green	*471, 469*	satin stitch
Streaked highlights	pink	*3608, 3607*	straight stitch, stem stitch

The embroidery sections and threads are listed in order of working. Repeat threads are shown in ***bold italics***.

Draw in the guide lines showing the angle of stitching with a transfer pencil, Fig 4.

4. Working the open flowers
Left: yellow/mauve pansy, right: pink pansy.

Mark the directional lines on the padding and follow them when working the long & short stitch. Note how the petals narrow towards the flower centre and reduce the number of long & short stitches as you work towards it.

The flower petals

6. Work the petals in **long & short** stitch from edge to centre. Follow the directional lines in Fig 4 and the shading of the finished embroideries. Work the dark mauve (550) streaks for the YELLOW/MAUVE PANSY in **straight** stitch.

The flower centres

The finished embroideries show two ways of working the centres of the open flowers.

7. For the YELLOW/MAUVE PANSY work in small **satin** stitches, Fig 5a. Use yellow (743) for the upper stitches, shown unshaded, and dark green (470) for the lower shaded ones.

8. For the PINK PANSY work a **French knot** with 3 or 4 strands of pale green (472), Fig 5b. Surround these with **seeding** stitches using a dark green (469).

Work pale pink (M0613) **bullion knots** either side of the centre to add highlights and depth.

  5. Working the flower centre

a. Yellow/mauve pansy. Work in small straight stitches, using yellow thread for the upper stitches and dark green for the lower, shaded, ones.

  b. Pink pansy. The centre of this flower is formed by a French knot, worked with 3 or 4 strands of pale green, surrounded by dark green seeding stitches. Pink Bullion knots on either side of the centre add depth.

Sepals

9. The sepals are formed as triangular **embroidered picots**, see Figs 6 to 8. The lower set of sepals must be embroidered first. It is impossible to work the embroidered picots over the long & short stitch of the petals, so the sepal triangles must be worked upwards from the base and turned down when finished.

Some of the upper sepals can be worked in **satin** stitch if you prefer.

Leaves & stems

10. Outline the edges of leaves in green (471) **split** stitch and fill the large leaves in **long & short** stitch. Work the central veins in **stem** stitch.

For the PINK PANSY only, work the small leaves in **satin** stitch and the small buds in **stem** stitch. Add the pink streaked highlights to the underside of the right leaf in **straight** stitch.

11. Work the stems in adjacent lines of **stem** stitch, shading the stitches as shown in the finished embroideries. For the PINK PANSY only, add the pink streaked highlights to the **stem** in stem stitch.

6. Pink pansy, larger bud
Working the lower sepals.

Note that the base of each picot is slightly slanted in relation to its petal, and overhangs it. Leave a small gap between the two picots at the base.

7. Pink pansy, larger bud
Completing the lower sepals.

Remove the pins from the two completed picots, Fig. 6, and turn them down over the top of the petals. Work a third picot across the top of the other two.

8. Pink pansy, larger bud
Working the upper sepals.

Turn down the third picot, Fig. 7, which will slightly overlap the other two. Work three smaller picots in the same way as the lower ones; make the outer ones first. Satin stitch may be used for some of the upper sepals.

Lilac

Designed and embroidered by the author

The little orchard at the end of the garden, carpeted with wild flowers and grasses, contains a small group of fruit trees, including the old Keswick codlin apple on p. 97. In May a pair of mauve lilacs give off their heady scent, their perfume so evocative of spring in an English garden.

With its heart-shaped leaves setting off the star-like single flowers, the lilac is very popular for beading and surface embroidery. It also provides excellent practice for your bullion knots. Embroidery actual size.

You will need

Embroidery hoop, 8 in (20 cm). Fine linen and cotton mixture, e.g. linen union or twill, 12 in (30 cm) square. Pink and mauve seed beads.
Threads: Appleton crewel wool (A); Anchor stranded cotton (An); Madeira silk (M).

Embroidery	Colour	Thread No	Stitches & effects
Leaves	grey-green	A352, 353, 355, 356	split, long & short stitch
Stems	grey-green	*as for leaves*	stem stitch
Veins	grass green	A251a	stem stitch
Branch	chocolate	A182, 184	stem stitch, French knots
Flowers	pink-mauve	An92, 94, 98, 99	satin stitch, bullion knots
	pink, mauve	M0503, 0613, 0801, 0803	
Flower centres and highlights	mauve	*M0801, 0803*	beading, French knots

The embroidery sections and threads are listed in order of working. Repeat threads are shown in ***bold italics***.

Embroidery notes

1. Transfer the outline and mount the fabric, see pp. 67, 106. The fabric needs to be a strong one. Tension the fabric over the hoop like a drum skin. Without sufficient tension the many **bullion knots** worked closely in the flower section can distort the fabric. Stitches and effects highlighted in the instructions in **bold** type are explained in detail under *Stitches & Techniques*.

The leaves, stems & branch

The leaves are worked entirely in wool to reproduce their matt appearance.

2. Outline the leaves in **split** stitch.

3. Work in **long & short** stitch from the outer edge towards the central vein. Follow the side veins to angle the stitches. As you are working from a wider space into a narrower one you need to reduce the number of stitches gradually. The flowers lying on top of leaves will be added later. Follow the embroidery as a guide to shading.

4. Work the central veins in green (A251a), the stems in grey-green, and the branch in chocolate, all in **stem** stitch. Add a few 2-stranded **French knots** at the base of each stem in chocolate.

The flowers

The four-petalled lilac flowers require special attention as they are worked in two layers within a small area. The lower layer is in **satin** stitch, with **bullion knots** round the edges as the upper layer, FIGS 1 - 6. Don't outline the petals.

5. First divide the threads listed for the flowers into light and dark. Choose any light pink or mauve, e.g. M0613 or 0801, and combine with any dark pink-mauve, e.g. An94 or 99.

If you want to use other threads you have within this colour range, pair them similarly. Keep the pairs together with an elastic band so you can always see which threads are paired. Work any given flower from the same pair, using the darker thread for the **satin** stitch and the lighter for the **bullion knots**.

6. Work each petal lengthways in **satin** stitch using the darker cotton thread, leaving a little space in the centre between them, FIG 1. Try to achieve evenly tensioned parallel stitches.

7. To create the raised edges work **bullion knots** in the lighter pink or mauve, using two strands of silk or three of cotton. Follow FIGS 2 - 6. You may wish to work some of the edges in **detached chain** stitch to add variety.

Leaving space in the centre of each flower (FIGS 1 & 6) avoids strain to the fabric through working all eight **bullion knots** into the same spot.

8. To finish add a seed **bead** to the centre of each flower, and a few between the flowers, to provide highlights. Alternatively **French knots** can be added to the centre or between the flowers.

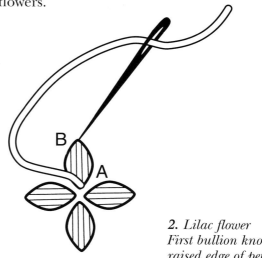

1. Lilac flower. The four petals with central space and directional lines.

Using a darker pink or mauve, work the petals lengthways in satin stitch.

2. Lilac flower First bullion knot for raised edge of petal.

Using a lighter pink or mauve, work the first of two bullion knots over the satin stitch. Bring the needle up at A, back down at B, and up again at A to make a bullion knot, which should be a little longer than the distance AB.

3. Lilac flower First complete bullion knot.

The bullion knot lies loosely between A & B.

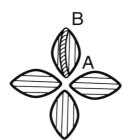

4. Lilac flower Forming the raised edge of a petal with a bullion knot.

Bring the needle up at C at the edge of the satin stitch area.

5. Lilac petal Securing the bullion knot along the edge.

Draw the bullion knot over to the left of the petal with a couching stitch, using the blunt edge of the needle to carry the thread under the knot. Reinsert the needle at C and pull the stitch taut to secure it. Work another bullion knot, repeating this procedure on the right of the petal.

6. Lilac flower with raised edges on all four petals.

Note the space left in the centre for a small bead.

Summer

Designed by the author, embroidered by Elsie Anna Burton

Nearly a century after Edith Holden's diary, her garden is now very much part of a town setting. Yet it remains an oasis of peace and tranquillity, full of the scents, sights and warmth of summer. Birds sing in the trees and dragonflies can be spotted darting in the sunlight over the pond.

There is a honeysuckle in full flower over a trellised arch, its scent filling the long evenings with sweet perfume. A buddleia, with its spikes of mauve flowers, acts like a magnet for the butterflies. There are wild roses, with their simple heart-shaped petals so inviting to the embroiderer, and a campanula, with small blue flowers that try each summer to creep into the house through the back door. Wild strawberries and purple heather grow in their weathered terracotta pots. Embroidery reduced size.

You will need

Embroidery hoop, 10 in (25 cm). Closely woven linen or satinised cotton, 14 in (35 cm) square. Green, gold and mauve-pink seed beads. Vilene padding. Threads: DMC stranded cotton.

Embroidery	Colour	Thread No
Honeysuckle leaves	green	3348, 3364, 3363, 3362
flowers	pink, red, green, yellow	3354, 3733, 3731, 3350, 742-745, 772
Rose leaves	yellow-green	472, 471, 470, 469
flowers	pink	819, 818, 776, 3326, 899, 335
centre	yellow, green, cream	*744*, 3820, *471, 469*, 3823
Heather stalks	green	*3364, 3363, 3362*
buds	mauve, purple	554, 553, 550
Strawberry leaves	yellow-green, green	*472, 471, 470, 469, 3362*
fruit	pink, red, brown, black	948, 353, 352, 351, 300, 898, 310
Campanula flowers	blue-mauve, white	3747, 341, 340, 3746, 333, 791, blanc neige
leaves	grey-green	504, 503, 502, 501, 500
Buddleia leaves	grey-green	*504, 503, 502, 501, 500*
flowers	mauve, purple	*3354, 554, 553*, 552, *550*

The embroidery sections and threads are listed in order of working. Repeat threads are shown in ***bold italics***.

Embroidery notes

Transfer the outline and mount the fabric, pp. 67, 105. Stitches and effects are listed with each part. They are highlighted in the instructions in **bold** type and explained in detail under ***Stitches & Techniques***.

Use the finished embroidery as a guide to shading. The project is worked from the centre of the design outwards, using single strands of thread except for **French** and **bullion knots**.

HONEYSUCKLE

Stitches & effects

Split stitch, padding, long & short, stem and running stitch, French & bullion knots, beading, straight stitch.

Leaves & stems

1. Outline the edges of the leaves in **split** stitch, in a mid-tone green. **Pad** the upper left and lower right leaves normally, then use FIGS 1 & 2 overleaf to pad the other two. Leave a narrowing gap along the central veins.

2. Work the leaves in **long & short** stitch following the shading from light to dark. Use the directional lines on the pattern as a guide for stitching (Fig 1, p. 42). Work the central veins in adjacent rows of light and dark green **stem** stitch.

1. Honeysuckle. Padding outline for leaf behind single campanula flower.

Pad only the unshaded section of the leaf.

2. Honeysuckle. Padding outline for right twisted leaf.

Do not pad the shaded underside.

3. Honeysuckle flower Enlarged petal; padding with running stitch.

Small running stitches worked at right angles to the edges of the petal provide an alternative light padding.

3. Work the stems in adjacent rows of **stem** stitch shading from left to right and light to dark. Use 3348, 3364, 3363.

The flower

The petals will be lightly padded with **running** stitches. Vilene cannot be used here as the split stitch filling would lie in the same direction as the split stitch outline and the outer rows would 'fall off' the edge of the padding!

4. Work rows of **running** stitch padding, Fig 3, stitching from side to side across the petals in a pale colour, such as cream.

Do *not* pad the shaded petals (Fig 1, p. 42) which are at the back and should appear less prominent.

5. Work along the petals in **split** stitch, across the rows of **running** stitch. Use reds and yellows to reflect the streaky shading of this flower.

6. Use **French knots** in 3 and 4 strands of yellows or green for the centre of the flower, with the darkest tones in the lower right area. Embroider the stamens in **stem** stitch, with a green seed **bead** for the stigma of the longest, and a small yellow **straight** stitch or **bullion knot** for the others.

WILD ROSE

Stitches & effects

Split stitch, padding, long & short stitch, French knots, straight stitch, beading, stem stitch.

1. Outline the edges of the petals and leaves in **split stitch** in a mid-tone thread of matching colour.

2. **Pad** the petals and leaves with a single layer of vilene, leaving a gap for the central vein, as shown in Fig 4.

3. Embroider the leaf stems in 2 or 3 closely worked adjacent rows of **stem** stitch, using the greens listed for the leaves. Shade from light on the left to dark on the right.

4. Work the leaves and the flower in **long & short** stitch. Follow Fig 4 for the angle of stitching.

5. Work the centre in yellow (744, 3820) and cream (3823) **French knots**. Use 2 and 3 strands and cluster the stitches closely.

6. From the centre radiate small **straight** stitches in yellow (3820) interspersed with a few in yellow-green (471, 469) to give shadow and depth.

7. Complete the rose with a few gold seed **beads** round the centre to represent stamen tips.

4. Wild rose. Guide to padding and angle of stitching

Pad all unshaded areas of the flower and leaves. Don't pad the shaded leaves or the narrow shaded strip where two leaves overlap.

Work the petals and leaves in long & short stitch, following the directional lines (petals) and side veins (leaves).

HEATHER

Stitches

Open fishbone stitch, straight stitch, fly stitch, detached chain stitch.

The heather in this design is interpreted slightly differently from others in the book. **Open fishbone** is still the basic stitch for the stems but **straight** and **fly** stitches have been added to give the plant more body, FIG 5.

5. Heather. General outline

Embroider the stems in open fishbone stitch. To add bulk, work a fly stitch or straight stitch where a leaf joins the stem.

Add **detached chain** and **straight** stitch in mauve and purple to represent the flowers.

STRAWBERRY

Stitches & effects

Split stitch, padding, long & short stitch, picots, bullion knots, beading, French knots, stem stitch.

Leaves & stems

1. The triple leaf is quite straightforward, FIG 6. First outline the edges and central veins in **split** stitch using a mid-green thread.

2. **Pad** the three leaf sections with a single layer, leaving a narrowing gap for central veins.

3. Work the leaf in **long & short** stitch following the directional lines. Embroider the three central veins in adjacent rows of **stem** stitch (472), starting with three rows at the base and reducing to one at the tip. Darker tones can be used to add shadow on the right and left-hand leaves.

The side veins in the embroidery were added in single rows of **stem** stitch (472, 469), but these are optional. Work the base of the leaves in a few radiating straight stitches (472), and the stem in adjacent rows of **stem** stitch, shading from light on the right to dark on the left.

6. Strawberry leaf Padding outline and angles of stitching.

Pad all the leaf sections, leaving gaps for the central veins. The side veins show the angles of stitching.

Berries

4. Now for the berries! Outline each berry in **split** stitch and apply two layers of **padding**, the smaller one first.

5. Embroider the berries in **long & short** stitch working in pinks and reds, shading from top to bottom and from light to dark. To add shadow to the sides of the berries work adjacent rows of **split** stitch.

6. Make the sepals as embroidered **picots** and **bullion knots** in green (471), FIG 7. The outer sepals are shown in side view.

7. Strawberry sepals & seeds

Work the two middle sepals in embroidered picots and the outer ones in bullion knots.

For the central seeds, sew translucent beads on a roughly diamond-shaped grid. Towards the sides, work smaller French knots closer together to give the right perspective. On the very edge, add shallow knots, shown on the outline by little bumps.

7. Use translucent yellow seed **beads** for the 'larger' seeds in front, and work the seeds towards the sides in **French knots**. Use two strands of brown (300, 898) for these **knots**, and black for those on the outline of the berry.

Don't follow the diamond shape of the grid too rigidly or the berries may look unconvincing.

8. Work all the stems in **stem** stitch and the basal leaves in **long & short** stitch in 472, 471 & 470.

CAMPANULA

Stitches & effects

Split stitch, padding, long & short stitch, straight stitch, satin stitch, stem stitch, bullion knots, beading.

These notes apply to the sprig of blue-mauve flowers on the left and the single flower at the centre front.

1. Outline the flowers and leaves in **split** stitch in mid-tone matching colours.

2. **Pad** all leaves and petals with a single layer, using FIG 8 as a guide, including the single flower at the bottom centre of the design.

3. Work the flowers and leaves in **long & short** stitch.

*9. Buddleia sprig
Padding outline for leaves.*

Pad only the unshaded areas and leave gaps in the padding for the central veins.

*8. Campanula
Padding outline.*

Pad all unshaded areas (petals and leaves) with a single layer, including the single flower at the bottom centre of the design.

4. Work the flower centres in **satin** stitch using dark blue (791) to create shadow. Use **stem** or **straight** stitch in white for the stamens, tipped with single gold seed **beads**.

5. Embroider the stems in **stem** stitch, and the buds in **bullion knots** interspersed with white highlights in **straight** stitch.

BUDDLEIA

Stitches & effects

Split stitch, padding, long & short stitch, stem stitch, detached chain stitch, satin stitch, straight stitch, bullion knots, fly stitch, French knots, beading.

1. Work the outlines of the leaves in **split** stitch in a mid-tone green, then **pad** the unshaded areas with a single layer, FIG 9.

2. Embroider the leaves in green **long & short** stitch following the directional lines in FIG 10.

3. Use **stem** stitch to work the main stem, which starts just above the honeysuckle. Shade from light to dark, left to right, using greens listed for the leaves.

4. Work the spiky side stems for the flowers, again in **stem** stitch, see FIG 10.

*10. Buddleia spray of flowers
Stitching the main and side stems.*

Work the main stem and the spiky side stems in stem stitch. Stagger the side stems along the main stem, reducing their length towards the tip.

5. Starting from the top add clusters of pink, mauve and purple flowers along the main stem, with some over the leaves. Position them so they appear to be growing from the side stems. You can have great fun adding tiny flowers!

6. The open flowers in the lower section have four petals. Work in **detached chain** stitch, **fly** stitch or **satin** stitch. If the petal centres in **detached chain** or **fly** stitch are open enough, they can be filled with **straight** stitches. Use mauve-pink seed **beads** or **French knots** for the flower centres.

7. Work the buds in **detached chain** stitch, with **satin** stitch or **straight** stitch centres. Some buds can be tiny **bullion knots** and some can have underside shadows of **fly** stitch, particularly upper buds.

Honeysuckle

Designed by the author, embroidered by Elsie Anna Burton.
Shown slightly reduced, and with its fabric guard devised by Barbara Cockerham, see p. 69 for details.

Honeysuckle

Designed by the author, embroidered by Elsie Anna Burton.
Fabric guard devised by Barbara Cockerham, see p. 69 for details.

This project has been extracted from 'Summer' to provide a special exercise in filling stitches. Although worked by the same embroideress, to the same design and with the same threads, the result is a picture of individual charm and character. Note the different shading of the petals, and the beading used for the flower centre. Embroidery slightly reduced.

You will need

Embroidery hoop, 5 in (12.5 cm). Closely woven linen or satinised cotton, 9 in (23 cm) square. Green seed beads. Vilene padding. Threads: DMC stranded cotton.

Embroidery	Colour	Thread No	Stitches & effects
Leaves	green	3364, 3363, 3362	split, long & short stitches, padding
Central vein	green	3348, *3362*	stem stitch
Stems	green	*3348, 3364, 3363*	stem stitch
Petals	pink, red, ecru, yellow, green	3354, 3733, 3731, 3350, ecru, 745-742, 772	running stitch padding, split stitch
Centre	green	*3364, 3363*	French knots, beading
Stamens	green, yellow	*3348, 3363, 742*	stem, straight stitches, beading

The embroidery sections and threads are listed in order of working. Repeat threads are shown in **bold italics**.

1. Pattern and padding outline
Pad only the unshaded leaves and petals.
See also Figs 2 & 3.

42

Embroidery notes

1. Transfer the outline and mount the fabric, see p. 67 and FIG 1 opposite. Stitches and effects highlighted in the instructions in **bold** type are explained in detail under *Stitches & Techniques*.

Use the finished embroidery as a guide to shading. Use single strands of thread unless otherwise stated.

Leaves & stems

2. Outline the edges of the leaves in **split** stitch, in a mid-tone green thread (3363). **Pad** the leaves except for the small underside section on the upper right tip, see FIGS 1 & 2. Leave a narrowing gap along the central veins.

3. Work the leaves in **long & short** stitch following the shading from light to dark. Use the directional lines on the pattern as a guide for stitching, FIG 1. Work the central veins in adjacent rows of light and dark green **stem** stitch.

4. Work the stems in adjacent rows of **stem** stitch, shading from left to right and light to dark. Use 3348, 3364, 3363.

The flower

The petals will be lightly padded with **running** stitches. Vilene and similar padding cannot be used here since the split stitch filling would lie in the same direction as the split stitch outline and the outer rows would 'fall off' the edge of the padding!

5. Work rows of **running** stitch padding, FIG 3, stitching from side to side across the petals in a pale colour, e.g. ecru.

Do *not* **pad** the shaded petals, FIG 1, which are at the back and should appear less prominent.

6. Work along the petals in **split** stitch, across the rows of **running** stitch. Use reds and yellows to reflect the streaky shading of this flower.

7. For the centre of the flower use **French knots** in 3 and 4 strands of greens, and green seed **beads**. Embroider the stamens in **stem** stitch, with a green seed **bead** for the stigma of the longest, and a small yellow **straight** stitch for the others.

2. Right twisted leaf, padding outline
Do not pad the shaded underside.

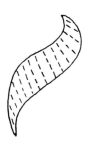

3. Enlarged petal, padding with running stitch
Small running stitches worked at right angles to the edges of the petal provide light padding.

Butterfly

Designed by the author, embroidered by Doris Ward.

Butterflies make terrible models as they tend to flutter off as soon as anyone appears with a sketch book or camera. But this fine tortoiseshell butterfly did obligingly settle on the buddleia in the garden just long enough to be drawn. Embroidery actual size.

You will need

Embroidery hoop, 4 in (10 cm). Closely woven cream linen, 8 in (20 cm) square. Vilene padding. Turquoise, black and brown seed beads. Threads: DMC stranded cotton; optionally Madeira silk (M).

Embroidery	*Colour*	*Thread No*	*Stitches & effects*
Wing outline	brick, mid-brown	920, 922	couching stitch, split stitch
Body outline	mid-brown	*922*	split stitch
Wing edges	mid-brown, peach, black	*922*, 402, 310	couching stitch stem stitch
Lower wing	yellow	3078	stem
Wing spots	yellow, black, mid-brown	*3078, 310, 922*	split stitch, satin stitch
Wing lines	grey	413	stem stitch
Upper wing	yellow, mid-brown	*3078, 922*	couching
Inner wing	mid-brown, bronze green-brown, black	*922*, 780, 610, *310*	long & short stitch, stem stitch
Upper body	green-brown, grey, mid-brown	*610, 413, 922*	padding, French knots
Lower body	mid-brown, bronze	*922* (M2209) *780* (M2213)	padding, bullion knots
Body tip	green-brown	*610*	straight stitch,
Antennae	green-brown	*610*	stem stitch, bullion/French knots
Markings			6 turquoise, 8 black seed beads
Eyes			2 brown seed beads

The embroidery sections and threads are listed in order of working. Repeat threads are shown in ***bold italics***.

Embroidery notes

1. Transfer the outline and mount the fabric, see pp. 67, 46. Stitches and effects highlighted in the instructions in **bold** type are explained in detail under ***Stitches & Techniques***. Use the finished embroidery as a guide to shading. Use single strands of thread unless otherwise stated.

Outlining & padding

2. Outline the outer left and right-hand edges of the wings in **couching** stitch in brick (920), carefully following the wing contours.

Use a single strand of couching thread to secure two strands of laid thread in the same colour, working at right angles to the laid thread. Follow the outlines carefully. If necessary work double couching stitches, one on top of another, to secure sharp changes of angle.

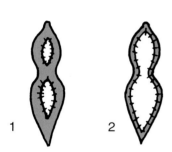

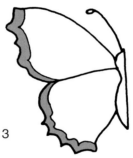

1. & 2. Butterfly body, guide to padding
Enlarged outline of the two stages.

Pad the unshaded areas and secure with small
overcast stitches. Always apply the smaller pieces first.

3. Butterfly wings, outer edge section
Work the shaded strip in 3 adjacent rows of couching.

3. Outline the body and remaining wing edges (including the mid dividing lines, FIG 3) in **split** stitch in the mid-brown (922) thread, easing each previous stitch back onto the outline with the next.

4. Pad the body only, in two layers, following FIGS 1 & 2. Apply the smaller pieces first, shown unshaded in FIG 1. Use overcast stitches to hold the padding in position. Add the second layer of **padding**, shown unshaded in FIG 2, again securing it with overcast stitches around the edges.

The wings

Follow FIGS 3 to 5, which show half the butterfly, applying the instructions to both halves.

5. Complete the outer edges of the wings (FIG 3) with two further adjacent rows of **couching**, next to the brick outline, using mid-brown (922) and peach (402). Follow the couching instructions in 2. above. This should fill the shaded area in FIG 3, but add extra stitches where necessary to fill gaps.

Pattern outline

6. Continue inwards to work the next section of the wings, shown shaded in FIG 4. Work this section in adjacent vertical rows of **stem** stitch in black. On the lower wing only, outline the inner edge with a single row of yellow **stem** stitch.

Stitch three turquoise seed **beads** to the upper wing, marked on the outline by circles.

7. To work the wing spots follow FIG 5. Start by outlining each spot in **split** stitch in a matching colour. The spots are worked in **satin** stitch: the small unshaded areas in yellow, and the black ones in black. The hatched area, worked in mid-brown, also indicates the direction of stitches on the upper part of the upper wing. For spots on the lower wing follow the angle of the dividing line between the wings.

8. To work the main wing areas and radiating lines follow FIGS 6 & 7. First embroider the radiating lines in grey **stem** stitch. In the narrow shaded area of the upper wing use two strands of yellow and **couch** them with a single strand of mid-brown.

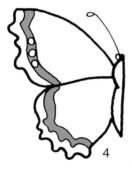

4. Butterfly wings
Working the next section.

Work the shaded strip in stem stitch or split stitch. On the lower wing only, outline the inner edge by a single row of yellow stem stitch. Add the three turquoise seed beads to this section, as shown by circles on the transfer.

5. Butterfly wings
Position of spots.

Work the spots in satin stitch: unshaded areas in yellow, black areas in black. The hatched area, worked in mid-brown, also indicates the direction of stitches on the upper wing. For spots on the lower wing follow the angle of the dividing line between the wings.

6. Butterfly wings
Radiating vein lines.

Work the lines in stem stitch, in grey thread. The thin shaded strip on the upper wing is worked with 2 strands of yellow, couched with a single strand of mid-brown.

9. Work the shaded areas of Fig 7 in **long & short** stitch. Work *between* the grey lines of stem stitch, which must remain well defined.

Work towards the body of the butterfly using shades from mid-brown (922), through bronze (780), and finally in deep green-brown (610) near the body. Decrease the numbers of stitches as the area narrows. Apply 4 small black seed **beads** to each upper wing for the spots: see the finished embroidery for the positions.

10. Work the small hatched section near the body at the angle shown in Fig 8. Use **long & short** stitch in streaks of mid-brown and deep green-brown. These sudden changes in tone simulate the downy texture of this surface. Tidy the edge and separate the area from the rest of the wing with a single line of black **stem** stitch. Separate off the upper and lower wings in the same way.

The body

11. Follow Fig 9 and work the upper part of the body in 2-stranded **French knots**, using grey and deep green-brown at the edges, mid-brown in the middle.

12. Work the lower section in 2 or 3-strand **bullion knots** with mid-brown and bronze threads. Alternatively they may be worked more easily in single-stranded silk.

13. Work three small **straight** stitches in green-brown to form the upper tip of the body, adding two small brown seed **beads** for the eyes. Try to position the eyes symmetrically on either side, or the poor creature may look cross-eyed!

14. Work the antennae in **stem** stitch, adding a tiny **bullion knot** or 2-stranded **French knot** at the tip, in green-brown thread.

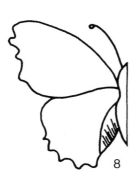

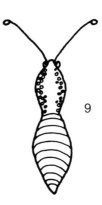

7. Butterfly wings. Main areas Work between the lines of grey in long & short stitch. Use mid-brown at the outer edges, bronze nearer the body and deep green-brown next to it. As the area narrows decrease the number of stitches.

8. Butterfly wings Downy section on lower wing.

Work the hatched area in long & short stitch, in streaks of mid-brown and deep green-brown. A single line of black stem stitch separates this section from the rest.

9. Butterfly body, enlarged to show areas of stitching

Work the upper part in 2-strand French knots, the lower in 2 or 3-strand bullion knots. Work three small straight stitches to form the body tip, with two small brown seed beads for the eyes. Work the antennae in stem stitch adding a tiny bullion knot or 2-stranded French knot at the tip.

47

Autumn

Designed and embroidered by the author.

The atmosphere of this 'season of mists and mellow fruitfulness' pervades our garden in autumn, and I have tried to reflect its mature richness in this design. For 'Autumn' I have gathered a stem of golden rod with its striking flowers, sorbus berries of red mountain ash and yellow Joseph Rock, crab apples, a small conifer sprig, and seed heads from open-centred marigolds. A cluster of cultivated blackberries from our thorny sprawling shrub completes the display.

Several methods of padding are used in this embroidery for the fruits and berries which are also used in traditional English stump work. Embroidery reduced size.

You will need

Embroidery hoop, 8 in (20 cm) and 4 in (10 cm). Linen union, 12 in (30 cm) square; calico for slips, 8 in (20 cm) square. Vilene padding; a little polyester stuffing (as in soft toys), or uncarded sheep's wool; white felt for the crab apples. Amber-yellow, black and deep red seed beads.

Threads: DMC stranded cotton (D); DMC retors à broder (RB); DMC coton perlé No 5(CP); Appleton crewel wool (A); Madeira silk (M).

Embroidery	*Colour*	*Thread No*
Golden rod flowers	golden yellow, light green, brown-olive	CP743, M1409, A312
Golden rod stem	grass green	A252
leaves	green, rust brown	*A252, M1409*, 2008
Mountain ash berries	salmon pink, red, rust brown	D3341, 351, M0402
Joseph Rock berries	yellow, sand	M0113, 0114, 2208
Mountain ash leaf, stem	green, red	M1309, 1311, *D351*
Conifer cones	brown	*M2008*
branch	green	*M1311*
Crab apples, leaves, stalks	sand, brown-olive	*M2208, A312*, 313
branch	grey	D645, 647
fruit	flesh pink, coral	M0306, A861, 862, 866
remains of sepal	black	D310
stalks	rust brown	*M0402*
Marigold, left seed head	salmon pink, rust brown, grey	*D3341, M0402, D645*, 647
right seed head	light green, rust brown	*M1409, 0402*
left stem	deep flesh pink	CP758
right stem	light green, salmon pink	*M1409, D3341*
leaves	light & grass green, rust	*M1409, A252, M0402*
Blackberries, stem	green, brown	RB2013, *M1309, 1311, 2008*
thorns	sand, rust brown	*M2208, 0402*
leaves	green, sand, rust brown	*M1309*, 1603, *1311, 2208, 0402*
raised & surface sepals	green	*M1309, 1311*
ripe berries	black, brown	*D310*, 838
unripe amber berry	sand	*M2208*
unformed open berry	flesh pink, brown	*M0306, D838*
unformed berry tip	brown	*D838*

The embroidery sections and threads are listed in order of working. Repeat threads are shown in ***bold italics***.

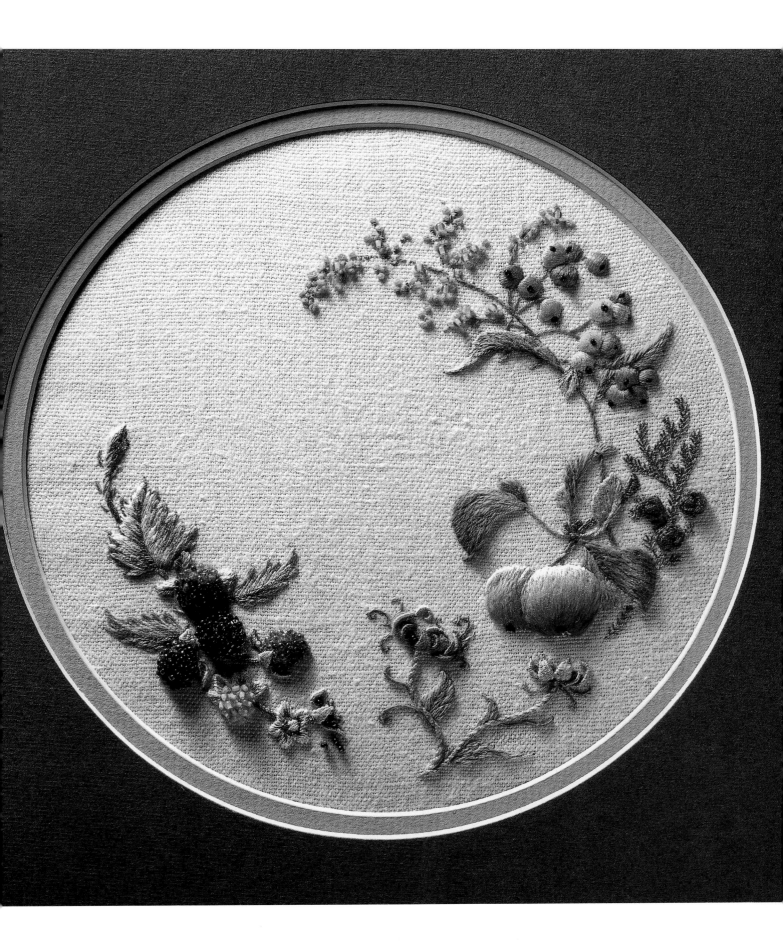

Embroidery notes

Transfer the outline and mount the fabric, see pp. 67, 109. Stitches and effects are listed with each part. They are highlighted in the instructions in **bold** type and explained in detail under *Stitches & Techniques*.

Use the finished embroidery as a guide to shading. Thread numbers are usually quoted in the text only when there is a choice of shades, so use the table to read off those you need for each section. The project is worked clockwise from the top. Work with single strands of thread throughout unless stated otherwise.

GOLDEN ROD

Stitches & effects

French knot, seeding stitch, beading, stem stitch, split stitch, long & short stitch.

1. Work the flowers in **French knots** using a single strand of yellow (CP743).

2. Mix in further **French knots** in light green silk (M1409) and brown-olive (A312). You can intersperse the knots with **seeding** stitches in the same colours.

3. Add further texture by applying about 18 amber-yellow seed **beads**. More are used in the unripe blackberry in the lower part of the picture, thus linking the two parts of the embroidery.

4. Work the stem in **stem** stitch.

5. Outline the leaves in **split** stitch (A252) and work them in **long & short** stitch, shading from light to dark.

SORBUS BERRIES

(MOUNTAIN ASH & JOSEPH ROCK)

Stitches & effects

Split stitch, padding, straight stitch, satin stitch, beading, French knots stem stitch.

1. Outline each berry in a matching colour in fairly small **split** stitches, easing each previous stitch back onto the outline to form a smooth curve.

2. Pad each berry with a small piece of loose polyester wadding squashed into a tiny ball (**alternative padding**, p. 98, FIG 1). Secure the edge of the ball with loosely worked **straight** stitches.

3. Embroider each berry with two layers of **satin** stitch. Work the upper layer at right angles to the one below (**alternative padding**, FIGS 2 & 3). Use salmon pink, red & rust for the clusters of red berries, and yellow & sand for the yellow ones.

4. To complete, stitch a small black seed **bead** or work a **French knot** tightly onto the berry. To create a 'natural' dip secure the bead with two stitches pulled tight.

5. Outline the leaves in **split** stitch (M1309). Work the leaf in **satin** stitch using both greens.

6. Work the stems in **stem** stitch (D351).

CONIFER SPRIG

Stitches & effects

Open fishbone stitch, banksia rose stitch.

1. Work the green conifer sprig in small **open fishbone** stitches using a single strand of dark green silk.

2. The three cones are worked in **banksia rose** stitches with two strands of brown silk.

CRAB APPLES

Stitches & effects

Split stitch, padding, long & short stitch, stem stitch, seeding stitch, French knots, straight stitch.

1. Outline the leaves in **split** stitch (M2208).

2. **Pad** the leaves as described in FIG 1. Work them in **long & short** stitch, starting from the edges and angling the stitches towards the central vein.

3. Work the leaf stalks in **stem** stitch (M2208), and the branch in closely-packed **seeding** stitches and **French knots**, which add texture.

4. Outline the little apples in **split** stitch (A861). To make a rounded profile, **pad** them with layers of white felt, see FIG 1.

50

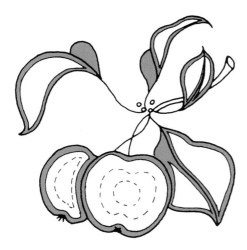

3. Flank the picots with **bullion knots**.

4. Work the outer curly lines in **split** stitch or **stem** stitch.

5. Make the **twisted cord** for the pink stem from one strand of coton perlé (CP758) twisted into two. Twist single strands of M1409 and D3341 to make the green and pink one.

Secure the cords as explained for **twisted cord** in *Stitches & Techniques*.

6. Work the broad leaves in **long & short** stitch and the thin curly ones in **stem** stitch.

2. Marigold seed heads

a. Simplified outline of left seed head.

• *Work the embroidered picot.*

• *Fold the picot back and add seed beads, French knots and French knots on stalks.*

• *Re-secure the picot over a single bead, see Fig. 2b.*

Work the side bullion knots, and the outer curly lines in split or stem stitch. Attach the twisted cord and secure with couching stitches.

b. Detail of picot.

Attach the point of the picot to the fabric with a small stitch, partly hiding one of the beads.

1. Crab apples. Padding outline

Pad unshaded areas of the leaves with vilene, and secure with overcast stitches.

Pad the fruit with felt: the whole apple with 3 layers, the other apple with 2. Start with the smallest layer, outlined in the middle, then add the next in size. Secure each layer with overcast stitches.

5. Embroider the apples in **long & short** stitch, starting at the bottom with the darkest thread and shading to the lightest at the top.

6. Work the residual sepals in black **straight** stitch and the stalks in **stem** stitch (M0402).

MARIGOLD SEED HEADS

Stitches & effects

Embroidered picots, beading, French knots, French knots on stalks, bullion knots, split stitch, stem stitch, twisted cord, couching, back stitch, long & short stitch.

1. Start by working the **embroidered picots**: one in the centre of the left seed head (M0402), FIG 2a, and two in the centre of the right seed head (M1409). The notes apply to both seed heads.

2. Pin the tips of the picots temporarily back towards the stalks. Sew on a few black seed **beads**, then work a few **French knots** and **French knots on stalks** at the centre of each seed head. Unpin the picots and curl them over the beads and knots. Secure the tip of each picot in a matching colour with a single small stitch, FIG 2b.

51

BLACKBERRIES

This spray is worked slightly differently from the *Blackberries* project opposite, but some diagrams are shared.

Stitches & effects

Split stitch, satin stitch, straight stitch, long & short stitch, embroidered picots, bullion knots, calico slips, beading, padding, French knots, French knots on stalks

1. *Main stem & side stalk.* Outline the wider end in **split** stitch (M1311), then **pad** the whole length in loosely-worked **straight** stitch (RB2013), see *Fig. 1* in *Blackberries*, p. 54. Cover in **satin** stitch up to the tip, including the cut end, using the three silk threads listed.

The stalk of the lower right berry is worked in **stem** stitch in two shades (M1309, 1311) The thorns are also in **stem** stitch.

2. *Leaves.* As the edges are serrated the leaves are not outlined. Embroider in **long & short** stitch from the central vein outwards. Add **straight** stitches (M0402) at the edges to give an autumnal tinge.

3. *Raised sepals.* Work these as **embroidered picots** *before* inserting the **calico slip** berries. Add side sepals as **bullion knots**. Flat sepals can be worked *before* or *after* the berries themselves.

4. *Flat sepals.* Outline the sepals in **split** stitch (M1309), and work in **satin** stitch (M1309), adding **straight** stitch shadows (M1311) from the centre, see FIG 4b.

5. *Ripe berries.* Prepare these separately in the smaller hoop as **calico slips**, p. 101, using mainly black but also some wine-red seed **beads**; cover the less ripe berries with more red than black ones. Fill the gaps between the beads with 2-stranded **French knots** and apply the finished berries to the fabric.

6. *Unripe amber berry.* This is **padded** only with felt. First work the flat sepals. To **pad** follow FIG 3. Apply amber seed **beads** interspersed with 2-stranded **French knots** (M2208).

3. Guide to padding the unripe berry in felt

Apply the smaller of the two pieces first and secure both with small overcast stitches.

7. *Unformed berry with open centre,* FIGS 4a & 4b. First work the sepals (as in *4.* above). Outline the centre in **split** stitch, lightly pad it with **seeding** stitches, and fill with **satin** stitch *over* the outline edge (all in M0306), FIG 4a. To finish surround the centre with tiny, *single*-stranded **French knots** (D838), FIG 4b.

8. *Unformed berry at the tip,* FIG 4c. Work the central sepal as an **embroidered picot** and the side ones as **bullion knots** (M1309), adding shadows on the inside in **straight** stitches (M1311). Unpin the **picot** and add several red and black seed **beads** and *single*-stranded **French knots on stalks** (D838). Secure the **picot** over the beads with a small stitch.

9. Apply 3 black seed **beads** in a triangle as shown.

4. Tip of blackberry stem
Berry with open centre.

a. *Outlining and working the centre.*

b. *Sepals with shadowing and completed centre with French knots.*

Berry at the tip.
c. Working the sepals and middle of berry.

Work the central sepal as an embroidered picot, then unpin the picot and add several seed beads and French knots on stalks. Curl the picot over the beads and secure it to the fabric with a stitch. Work a bullion knot on either side and complete with three black seed beads sewn in a triangle.

Blackberries

Designed by the author, embroidered by Doris Ward.

Blackberries have proved so popular with embroiderers that I have extracted these from the main 'Autumn' embroidery as a special 'mini'-project. The design is the same, but the treatment and shading are different.

Embroidery actual size.

See also enlarged berries, pp 95, 101.

You will need

Embroidery hoops, 6 in (15 cm) and 4 in (10 cm).

Closely woven linen, 10 in (25 cm) square; calico for slips, 8 in (20 cm) square.

Small piece of felt, red or brown; polyester stuffing, or uncarded sheep's wool. Red, wine red and black seed beads.

Threads: DMC stranded cotton (D); DMC retors à broder (RB); Madeira silk (M).

Embroidery	Colour	Thread No	Stitches & effects
Stem, thorns	brown, khaki, ecru	D3776, 400, RB2839, ecru	stem, split stitch, straight, satin stitch
Leaves	green, brown	M1309,1603,1311, 2208,0402, D3776	long & short, straight stitch
Central veins	brown	*D400*	stem stitch
Raised sepals	green	*M1309*	picots, bullion knot
Flat sepals	green	*M1309, 1311*	split, satin, straight stitch
Ripe berries	black, brown	D310, 838	calico slips, beading, French knot
Unformed berry	green, brown	*M1309, D400, 838*	split, satin, seeding stitch, French knot
Unripe berry	green	*M1309*	picot, bullion knot, alt. padding, beading

The embroidery sections and threads are listed in order of working. Repeat threads are shown in ***bold italics***.

Embroidery notes

1. Transfer the outline and mount the fabric, see pp. 67, 55. Stitches and effects highlighted in the instructions in **bold** type are explained in detail under *Stitches & Techniques*.

Use the finished embroidery as a guide to shading. Use single strands of thread throughout, except where stated otherwise.

The stem

2. Start by working the stems: first the thin ones, nearer the tip, in **stem** stitch (D3776, 400).

3. Outline the wide upper section of stem in **split** stitch (D3776) then **pad** it with loosely-worked **straight** stitches (RB2839), FIG 1. If you have difficulty in drawing the thick padding thread through the fabric, make a small hole first with a large needle or stiletto.

1. Wide end of stem: guide to light padding in retors à broder

After outlining in split stitch, pad with loosely-worked straight stitches, shown shaded. They can be couched lightly at intervals with sewing thread or a strand of cotton.

4. Embroider this section in two stages: first from the middle to the end, returning to the middle to complete it in the other direction. Work in slanted **satin** stitch at the angle shown in FIG 2, over the **split** stitch outline. To maintain the correct angle of stitches along the curve, follow instructions in FIG 2.

5. Cover the cut end of the stem in **split** stitch in ecru, following the broken lines in FIG 2. Add the thorns in **straight** stitch (D400).

Leaves

6. As the leaves have serrated edges they are not outlined. Embroider in **long & short** stitch from the central vein outwards. **Straight** stitches in brown (D3776) can be worked here and there at the edges to add an autumnal look. Outline the central veins in **stem** stitch (D400).

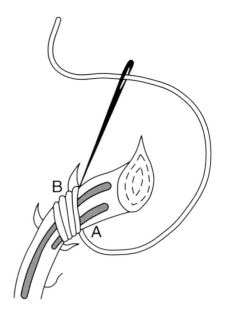

2. Working satin stitch over the wide end of the stem

Work in two stages: first from the middle to the end, then returning to the middle to complete it in the other direction. Work the slanted satin stitch over the split stitch outline, as shown.

To maintain the correct angle along the curve, keep the ends of stitches on the inner edge A closer together, while spreading them fractionally at the outer edge B.

Sepals

7. The raised sepals must be embroidered *before* inserting the calico slip berries. Make them as **embroidered picots** and **bullion knots** in green (M1309).

8. The flat sepals can be worked *before* or *after* the berries have been attached. Outline them in **split** stitch (M1309), and work them in **satin** stitch (M1309) adding **straight** stitch shadows at the centre (M1311).

Calico slip berries

9. Prepare the ripe berries separately in the smaller frame as **calico slips**, p. 101. Add black and wine-red seed **beads** and fill the gaps between the beads with 2-stranded **French knots**. Apply the finished berries to the fabric.

10. For the unformed berry, FIG 3, outline the sepals in **split** stitch (M1309) and work them in **satin** stitch.

Outline the centre in **split** stitch, lightly pad it with **seeding** stitches, and work in **satin** stitch (D400). Surround the centre with tiny, single-stranded **French knots** (D838).

3. *Unformed berry*
Outline each sepal in split stitch and fill with satin stitch in the direction of the single line.

Outline the centre, lightly pad it with seeding stitches and fill it with satin stitch over the outlined edge.

Angle the satin stitch as shown by the directional lines. Work single-stranded French knots around the centre.

11. The unripe berry at the tip of the stem is not worked as a calico slip, but padded with felt (see **alternative padding**). First work the sepals (M1309): the central one is an **embroidered picot**, flanked on either side by a **bullion knot**. Pin back the finished picot temporarily, away from the base of the berry.

4. *Unripe berry at tip of stem*
Guide to padding in felt.

First apply the smaller oval, outlined by the broken line, then the larger one, and secure each to the embroidery fabric with small overcast stitches. Apply red seed beads onto the felt.

Cut two oval layers of felt, FIG 4, and apply first the smaller, then the larger one. Secure each layer with **overcast** stitches. Stitch red seed **beads** closely together onto the felt. Unpin the **picot** and curl it back over the berry. Secure the tip to the berry with a stitch for a closed effect.

12. Stitch 3 black seed **beads** in a triangle as shown.

Pattern outline

Autumn bouquet

Designed and embroidered by the author.

At the centre of this design is the bicoloured rose 'Masquerade', with its blend of soft yellows and reds. The rose was drawn during its second flowering, in October. Here it is set among Michaelmas daisies, heather, honeysuckle berries – much loved by the birds – and thalictrum leaves, already gold in expectation of their fall.

The design makes full use of a wide range of colours, from warm yellow to purple, and the silvery grey-green of the rose leaves provides a perfect foil for these autumnal tints, but you can use any stranded cotton threads in your collection which harmonise with the colours shown. Embroidery reduced size.

You will need

Embroidery hoop, 8 in (20 cm). Closely woven linen, 12 in (30 cm) square.

Threads: Anchor stranded cotton (An); DMC stranded cotton (D)

Embroidery	*Colour*	*Thread No*
Michaelmas daisy, petals	mauve	An95, 96, 98, 99
stamens, sepals	cream, yellow, yellow-green	An292, 295, 279, 280
leaves, stems	yellow-green	*An279, 280*, 281
Honeysuckle, berries	peach, red, brown-red	An323, 332, D3721
berry highlights	cream	An275
stem	yellow-green	*An279, 280*
Heather, flowers	purple	An94, *99*
stem, leaves	green	An266
Thalictrum, stem	rust brown	D783
leaves	fawn, rust brown	D676, *783*
Cotoneaster, berries	cream, yellow, red, brown-red	*An292, 295, 332, D3721*
leaves, stem	yellow-green	*An279, 280, 281*
separate berries, leaves	rust brown, fawn	*D783, 676*
Rose, petals	cream, yellow, gold, pink, rust	*An292, 295*, 298, D760, 3712, *783*
shadow	brown-red, green	*D3721, An266*
stamens & centre	cream, rust brown	*An292, D783*
leaves, stems	grey-green	An213, 859, 262
small touches on leaves	green	*An266*

The embroidery sections and threads are listed in order of working. Repeat threads are shown in **bold italics**.

Embroidery notes

Transfer the outline and mount the fabric, see pp. 67, 59. Stitches and effects are listed with each part. They are highlighted in the instructions in **bold** type and explained in detail under *Stitches & Techniques*.

Use the finished embroidery as a guide to shading. Thread numbers are usually quoted in the text only when there is a choice of shades, so use the table to read off those you need for each section. The project is worked clockwise, starting from the Michaelmas daisies at the top. Use single strands of thread throughout except for the French knots which require two.

MICHAELMAS DAISIES

Stitches

Straight stitch, French knots, detached chain stitch, stem stitch, close fishbone stitch, satin stitch, fly stitch.

1. Work the petals in **straight** stitch, radiating outwards from the stamens. To create shadow use the darker tones of mauve and slightly shorter stitches.

2. Work the stamens in cream, yellow and yellow-green (An292, 295, 279) **French knots**, and the shadows in yellow-green (280). Work the sepals in **detached chain** stitch (An279, 280).

3. Stems are worked in **stem** stitch; the main leaves can be worked in either **close fishbone** stitch or **satin** stitch, and the smallest leaves in **fly** stitch.

HONEYSUCKLE BERRIES

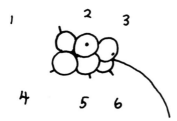

Stitches

Split stitch, satin stitch, straight stitch, French knots, long & short stitch, stem stitch.

1. Follow FIG 1. Start from the edge of each berry. Embroider berries *2 & 3*, and all berries in the right-hand cluster, in concentric rings of small **split** stitches. Graduate from the darkest brown-red (D3721) on the edges to the lightest at the centre. Add three or four cream **satin** stitches to the centre to provide highlights.

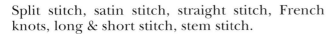

1. Honeysuckle berries, left cluster
Berries 2 & 3 are worked in concentric rings of small split stitch; berries 1,4, 5 & 6 in long & short stitch.

2. Using the same colours work berries *1, 4, 5 & 6* in **long & short** stitch. The little dark spikes are worked in brown-red **straight** stitches (D3721) or 2-stranded **French knots**.

3. Work the stem in **stem** stitch.

HEATHER

Stitches

Open fishbone stitch, detached chain stitch, French knots.

Work the stem and leaves in **open fishbone** stitch, and the flowers in **detached chain** stitch and **French knots**.

THALICTRUM LEAVES

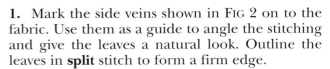

Stitches

Split stitch, stem stitch, long & short stitch.

1. Mark the side veins shown in FIG 2 on to the fabric. Use them as a guide to angle the stitching and give the leaves a natural look. Outline the leaves in **split** stitch to form a firm edge.

2. Define the central veins in **stem** stitch (D783). Starting from the edges, work the leaves in **long & short** stitch, using brown (D783) near the edges and the lighter (D676) near the central vein.

3. Work the stems in **stem** stitch.

2. Thalictrum leaf, guide to stitching
Outline the leaf in split stitch and mark the veins on the fabric. Use the side veins to angle the long & short stitches.

COTONEASTER BERRIES

Stitches

Split stitch, long & short stitch, French knot, stem stitch, satin stitch, close fishbone, fly stitch.

1. Outline all three berries in red (An332) in small **split** stitches. Work the two lower berries in **long & short** stitch and the upper berry in concentric rings of **split** stitch from dark at the edges to light in the centre.

2. Work a single-stranded **French knot** (D3721) for each dark spot.

3. Work the stem in **stem** stitch (D280) and the leaves in **satin** stitch using the three shades.

4. Work the tiny berries between the Michaelmas daisies in rust brown (D783) **satin** stitch, and the pale leaves next to them in **close fishbone** and **fly** stitch (D676).

ROSE

Stitches

Split stitch, long & short stitch, French knots on stalks, French knots, whipped spider web stitch, stem stitch.

1. *The flower.* Mark the directional lines on the petals as shown in FIG 3. Outline each petal in split stitch. Work the petals in **long & short** stitch, starting at the edge and working towards the centre. Gradually reduce the stitches per row to fit the narrowing space.

Use the darker tones listed for areas of shadow cast by the petal in front.

2. Work the stamens in **French knots on stalks**, in rust brown (D783), and single-stranded **French knots** in cream (An 292). Embroider the centre in a **whipped spider web** stitch, also in cream.

3. *Leaves.* Do *not* outline the edges as these leaves should not stand out. Work them in **long & short** stitch starting from the central vein. Add the highlights as shown in light green (An266).

3. Rose, guide to stitching

Mark the directional lines of the petals onto the fabric as a guide for stitching.

Define the central veins in **stem** stitch where shown in grey-green (An 262).

4. Work the stems in **stem** stitch using the three listed shades.

Pattern outline

Christmas

Designed by the author, embroidered by Barbara Cockerham.

This small project has been adapted from 'Winter' and uses the same techniques, threads and shading. Working notes for each section can be found in 'Winter' itself. Embroidery actual size.

Stitches & effects

WINTER JASMINE

Stem stitch, split stitch, padding, long & short stitch, straight stitches, beading, detached chain stitch.

COTONEASTER

Stem stitch, split stitch, long & short stitch, satin stitch, French knots, beading.

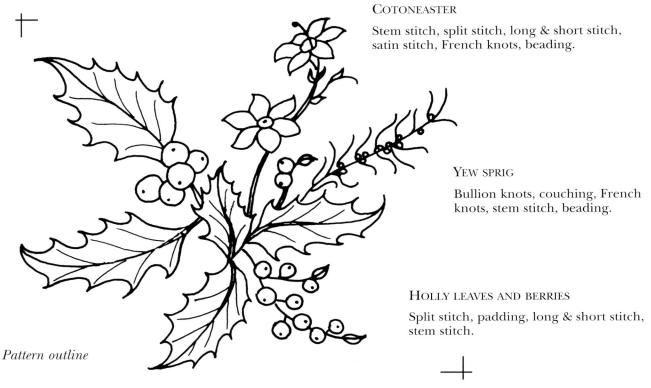

YEW SPRIG

Bullion knots, couching, French knots, stem stitch, beading.

HOLLY LEAVES AND BERRIES

Split stitch, padding, long & short stitch, stem stitch.

Pattern outline

You will need

Embroidery hoop, 6 in (15 cm). Closely woven linen or cotton, 10 in (25 cm) square.
Black, off white or pearl, and gold seed beads. Vilene padding. Threads: DMC stranded cotton.

Embroidery	Colour	Thread No
Jasmine flowers	yellow, green	445, 307, 471
stems	green	472, *471*, 470
Yew leaves	green	369, 368, 320, 367, 319
flowers	ecru	ecru
Cotoneaster berries	pink, red, black	761, 760, 3328, 347, 310
leaves & stems	green, khaki-brown	*471, 470*, 611
Holly berries	pink, red, black, white	754, 352, 351, 817, *310*, blanc neige
leaves	grey-green, ecru	524, 523, 522, 520, ecru

The embroidery sections and threads are listed in order of working. Repeat threads are shown in ***bold italics***.

Stitches & Techniques

This part of the book provides comprehensive support for the embroiderer working projects in surface embroidery and includes some raised embroidery techniques. In particular it explains in detail the stitches and effects highlighted in **bold** *type in the projects. It is subdivided into*

- *materials & equipment 66*
- *starting the embroidery 70*
- *line stitches 71*
  stem, split, running, couching stitches
- *knotted stitches 74*
  French knots & knots on stalks, bullion knots
- *looped stitches 80*
  detached & continuous chain, fly, open & closed fishbone stitches
- *filling stitches 85*
  long & short, satin, whipped spider web, seeding, straight stitches
- *surface effects 94*
  beading, padding, picots, banksia rose stitch, calico slip, twisted cord

Individual stitches are listed on the Contents page at the beginning of the book.

The embroideries in this part are intended to illustrate the stitches and techniques described next to them. Their pattern outlines are included with the other project outlines at the end of the book. Additional small pattern outlines are included within the text as practice exercises.

Sampler

Designed by the author, embroidered by Elsie Anna Burton.

This design was drawn after an August country walk and uses the soft yellows and golds, mellow greens and warm browns so typical of this season. The embroidery includes most of the stitches and some of the surface effects explained later in detail. Embroidery reduced size.

Embroidery notes

Transfer the pattern outline using red, orange or yellow dressmakers' carbon paper instead of the normal blue, pp. 67, 110.

Use satinised cotton or closely-woven linen and work with stranded cotton threads from your collection. Use single strands throughout except for **French knots** and **bullion knots** which require 2 or 3 strands. If you find bullion knots difficult to work in stranded cotton, single-stranded Madeira silk can be used instead.

Work down from the top using the stitches listed.

Key to stitches and surface effects

LINE STITCHES

1. ***Stem stitch*** *– stems of daisy, cow parsley, poppy seed head, etc; shadow under and between grains of oats; as a filling for wheat leaf.*

2. ***Split stitch*** *– underlying outline stitch for oats, wheat, twisted grass, daisy petals, poppy seed heads; as a filling for lower sections of twisted grass.*

3. ***Couching stitch*** *– wheat stems.*

KNOTTED STITCHES

4. ***French knots*** *– oilseed rape, daisy centres.*

5. ***French knots on stalks*** *– cow parsley.*

6. ***Bullion knots*** *– clover flower.*

LOOPED STITCHES

7. ***Detached chain stitch*** *– tops of upper left and lower right poppy seed heads.*

8. ***Continuous chain stitch*** *– edging of central right poppy seed head.*

9. ***Open fishbone stitch*** *– yarrow.*

10. ***Close fishbone stitch*** *– clover leaves.*

FILLING STITCHES

11. ***Long & short stitch*** *– wheat, upper section of twisted grass, lower section of poppy seed heads, daisy petals.*

12. ***Satin stitch*** *– grains of oats.*

13. ***Whipped spider web stitch*** *– top of a poppy seed head.*

14. ***Straight stitch*** *– tips of wheat ears.*

SURFACE EFFECTS

15. ***Padding (vilene)*** *– grains of wheat, oats, oilseed rape, daisy centres.*

In preparation

Materials and equipment

Fabrics

A firm closely-woven fabric is ideal for embroidering in stranded cotton. Pure linen, sometimes called 'church linen', is best but more expensive, and a good alternative is satinised cotton. This is a fairly thick closely-woven cotton which was used for the *Sampler*.

A linen or cotton woven slightly more openly is needed for embroideries worked in crewel wool, such as linen union or linen/cotton twill.

Evenweave linen and cotton sold for counted thread embroidery are too loosely woven, and synthetic fabrics should also be avoided.

Threads

The threads used are stranded cotton, coton perlé, retors à broder, silk, and crewel wool. Your embroideries do not have to be exact replicas of the examples illustrated, so there is no need to buy a complete set of new threads for each new project. You may already have a collection of threads, some of which – with discretion – can be used. Your threads should be bleed-proof, in case you wish to wash your work.

This type of embroidery also offers you the chance to interpret a design in your own way, not least in the choice of threads, but you must ensure that your choice looks well together. Start by laying out your collection, colour by colour. For areas that include long & short stitch ensure you have a run of shades from light to dark in the colours required, see skeins of embroidery thread on *Apples* p. 97. This is most important.

A good working length of thread is from the tip of your fingers to your elbow. Threads cut too long will tangle, knot or even break during working.

To work with more than one strand of stranded cotton, cut a working length from the hank: this contains 6 strands. If you require only 3 strands, for example, separate 3 strands individually from the working length. Then, holding the strands together at one end between one thumb and forefinger, slide the thumb and forefinger of the other hand gently along the length of the threads so that they lie evenly side by side. Your thread is now ready for use.

Stranded silk threads should be prepared in the same way.

When mixing **long & short** stitches in silk with stitches in crewel wool, work the silk before the wool if possible as the threads will blend better.

Needles

For this type of work use crewel or embroidery needles. They have long slim eyes, which allow the thread to pass through the fabric without shredding, and are relatively easy to thread.

For single-stranded cotton thread use a fine needle. For more than one strand a slightly thicker needle is necessary. For silk or wool a medium needle is required. A tapestry needle is recommended for one section of whipped spider web stitch and extra fine needles are needed for beading. The larger the number of the needle the smaller the eye.

Thread	Needle size
Embroidery cotton, 1 strand	No 10
Embroidery cotton, 2-4 strands	No 9
Coton perlé No 5	Nos 3-5
Retors à broder	No 3
Madeira silk, single strand	No 9
Madeira silk, double strand	No 7
Appleton crewel wool	Nos 3-5
Beading thread and Sylko 40 dressmaking thread	No 10 or beading needle

Pins

You will need dressmaker's pins for anchoring paper patterns or embroidered picots, and for holding padding in place.

Scissors

Small sharp embroidery scissors are essential. You will find a range of good modern ones available, but don't discard the old steel type, like the pair in the *Apples* embroidery. These are most effective if kept sharp.

You will need a larger pair of dressmaking scissors for cutting fabrics.

Tracing paper and other papers

Use *tracing paper* to trace your patterns, and *dressmaker's carbon paper* to transfer the traced outline to the fabric. For light fabrics use a dark colour, e.g. dark blue, but avoid secretarial carbon paper which will stain your fabric. *Acid free tissue paper* is used to protect the edges of the embroidery fabric from finger marks: see *Mounting the fabric*, p. 68 and *Apples*, p. 97.

Embroidery frames

The best type of frame supports the embroidery independently, freeing both hands to work the needle. These include frames with a seat, and versions which can be clamped to a table.

Every embroidery in this book has been worked on a hoop frame, also known as a 'tambour' or 'ring' frame. They are available in various sizes, from 4 inch (10 cm) up to 12 inch (30 cm), and are made of two hoops, one inside the other: the outer one usually has a screw clamp. The inner hoop must be tightly bound with straight white tape, see *Fig. 1*, p.68.

Transfer pencil

This is a soft marker pencil, usually blue or mauve, which must be kept *sharp*. Use it to mark in the direction of stitching for patterns with long & short stitch or other filling stitches.

Beads

Modern seed beads come in various sizes and a wide range of colours. The smallest are particularly useful for stamens, and slightly larger ones for fruits such as the blackberries on pages 91 & 101. Beads should be applied with a fine crewel or beading needle.

Padding

The main padding used in this book is a synthetic interlining, $1/16$ in (1.6 mm) thick and about 200 gsm in density, sold in Britain as extra heavy sew-in Vilene. For alternatives abroad see *Suppliers,* p. 112. Felt or its synthetic alternative polyester felt (e.g. Thermalan), loose polyester wadding (as used in soft toys), and sheep's wool (from pharmacists) are also used for special effects. Felt will shrink if you wash your work, but vilene and polyester felt will not.

Aligning the pattern

Alignment lines appear on each pattern outline. Make sure they are aligned with the warp and weft of the fabric before transferring the pattern.

Transferring the pattern onto the fabric

1. Follow FIG 1. Photocopy your pattern onto tracing paper or trace the outline by hand onto good quality tracing paper using an HB pencil, including the alignment lines, and directional lines for stitching (where shown).

2. Cut the fabric to size, allowing at least 2 in (5 cm) all round the design plus a minimum of 2 in (5 cm) outside the hoop for stretching.

3. Press the fabric and lay it, right side up, on a clean hard surface.

4. Place the traced outline over the centre of the fabric and align with the warp and weft using the alignment lines on the pattern.

5. Pin the tracing in place.

6. Slip a piece of dressmaker's carbon paper (dark blue for pale fabrics) *face down.*

7. Retrace the outline but don't transfer the alignment lines.

You may wish to replace the hidden area beneath the mount by a border of cheaper firm fabric, e.g. calico. Machine stitch the extensions to each edge, ensuring the warp and weft of both fabrics lie in the same direction. Zigzag or over

sew the outer edges to prevent them from fraying while the embroidery is in progress.

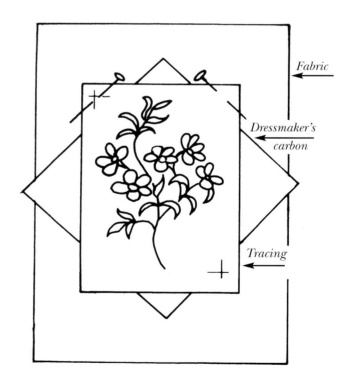

1. Transferring the pattern onto the fabric

Position the tracing over the centre of the fabric with the alignment lines along the warp and weft. Secure with two pins. Slip the dressmaker's carbon paper, face down, between tracing and fabric. Trace the design with an HB pencil or a spent fine ball-point pen.

Mounting the fabric

To mount the fabric in an embroidery hoop you will need white $1/2$ in or 15 mm cotton tape and acid-free tissue paper. Bias binding is unsuitable.

1. Follow FIG 1. Bind the inner hoop tightly with the tape, working at an angle and overlapping the edges slightly, as shown. Work evenly round the ring keeping the tape under tension.

2. Stitch the two ends neatly together to prevent unwinding.

3. Lay the inner hoop on a flat clean surface and place the fabric on top with the traced design face up. Centre the design carefully over the hoop.

4. Place a piece of acid free tissue paper over the fabric.

5. Loosen the screw on the outer hoop and press it down carefully over the inner hoop, sandwiching the tissue paper and fabric between the two.

6. Tighten the screw a little to hold the fabric in place and tension the fabric evenly so that it is stretched like a drum across the inner hoop.

7. Check from below that no ripples remain on the fabric, and when it is taut enough finally tighten the screw. A well-tensioned fabric is *essential* for good results.

8. With the point of a needle, lightly score the tissue paper all round the hoop, about an inch (2.5 cm) in from the rim. Tear away the centre: the outer rim of tissue paper will protect the fabric from finger marks, and prevent the outer hoop from marking the fabric, see *Apples*, p. 97. This will save washing the finished embroidery.

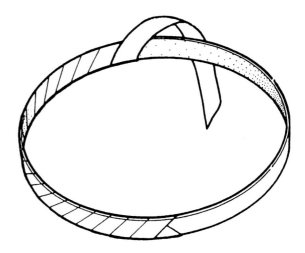

1. Binding the inner hoop

Use white $1/2$ in (15 mm) wide tape. Work at an angle and overlap the edges slightly as you proceed round the frame. Stitch the ends carefully together on the inside of the hoop.

Tips and suggestions

Tracing the pattern outline. Photocopy the pattern outline twice, once onto tracing paper and once onto normal paper.

Use the copy on tracing paper instead of tracing the outline by hand.

Use the paper copy to cut out the shapes needing padding, except where a padding outline is included with the project. Lay the cut-out pattern over the padding material and cut it out fractionally smaller than the pattern: this will produce an accurate shape for padding.
Suggested by Elsie Anna Burton.

Finding the right working angle. If you find stitches such as **stem** stitch and **satin** stitch difficult to work at certain angles, turn your hoop and work at an angle you find comfortable.

For left-handed embroiderers. When working **French knots** and **bullion knots** view the diagrams in a mirror. This will reverse the hand into the right position for you.

Avoiding threads tangling. If you are working with several threads, leave any you are not using on top of the fabric, see *Apples*, p. 97. If you leave them underneath they may get tangled up. If you use a fabric guard they can be tucked into it.

Your own mini project. You may wish to use part of a larger embroidery as a small project of your own. To do this, copy and cut out the section you would like to use from the pattern outline. Move it around on a sheet of white paper until you find a pleasing arrangement. Tape or glue it in position, add the alignment lines showing the direction of warp and weft, and copy it again to use as your mini project outline.

The hoop cover or fabric guard

This device, shown on p. 41, lies over the protective paper ring described in *Mounting the fabric* opposite. It gives increased protection for the most handled part of the fabric and provides a convenient pocket to tuck away fabric lying under the hoop, and working threads not in use above it. It also helps keep the fabric tensioned.

Calico, cotton or polyester/cotton are suitable materials for this cover. Follow FIGS 1 & 2. Start with a rectangular strip of fabric. For the length, measure the circumference of your embroidery hoop, including the screw, and add $1\frac{1}{4}$ in (30 mm). For the width take the hoop thickness plus 4 in (10 cm). Join the short edges of the fabric together to form a band with a $\frac{5}{8}$ in (1.6 cm) seam allowance.

Check that the band fits snugly around the hoop and adjust the seam if necessary. Make hems along both long edges and thread narrow elastic through them. The result should fit over your hoop like a cover over a car steering wheel, see FIG 2 below and *Honeysuckle*, p. 41.
Devised by Barbara Cockerham.

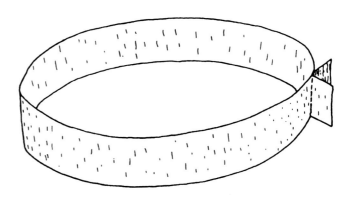

1. Making the hoop cover

The length of fabric corresponds to the hoop circumference, including the screw, + $1\frac{1}{4}$ in (30 mm); the width is the thickness of the hoop + 4 in (10 cm). Stitch the ends of the fabric strip to form a band.

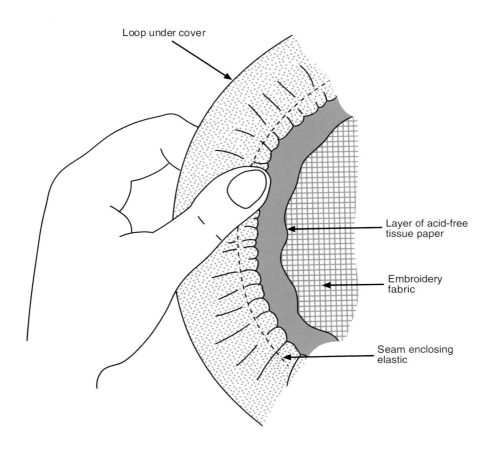

Loop under cover

Layer of acid-free tissue paper

Embroidery fabric

Seam enclosing elastic

2. Detail of the finished hoop cover

The broken line shows the upper seam for the elasticised edge. The inner line shows the edge of the tissue paper.

Starting the embroidery

In surface embroidery the thread is initially secured by means of a waste knot, though not in every case. Some stitches, **bullion knots** and **French knots** on stalks for example, are begun with an alternative method given below.

Starting with a waste knot

See Figs 1 to 4. This example is for starting in stem stitch from the base of a stem, but can be used for other stitches. The waste knot is inserted at *A*, some way up the stem, and the needle is brought up at the base, *B*, from which stem stitch is worked. Once this has secured the thread beneath, the waste knot is cut off as waste.

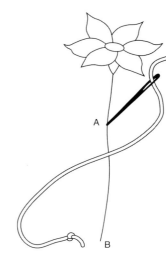

1. Starting with a waste knot

Make a knot and insert the needle at A, at least three stitches away from the base B. Bring up the needle at B.

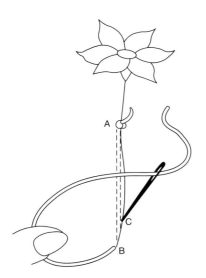

2. The first securing stitch

Secure a loop of thread with your left thumb and insert the needle at C on the stem. The stem, slightly curved, is shown by a solid line. The thread to be secured beneath the fabric, held in position by the waste knot, is shown by broken lines. It may not follow the line of the stem.

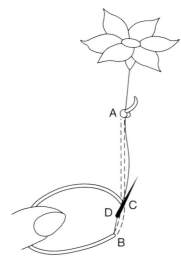

3. Completing the securing stitch

Use the tip of the needle to push the thread lying beneath the fabric to the side of the stem line and bring up the needle at D. Release your thumb from the loop and pull up the needle. Make at least two more stitches up the stem line. After three consecutive securing stitches cut off the waste knot.

4. The first securing stitch seen from below
The stitch between C and D secures the thread beneath the fabric.

Starting with a back stitch

This method is suitable for starting **bullion knots** and **French knots on stalks**. Begin with one tiny **back** stitch – or two worked one on top of the other – to secure the end of the thread, Fig 5. Back stitch is a basic stitch related to **stem** stitch. It is also used to finish surface effects such as the **twisted cord**.

Another method is to run the thread behind previous stitches and work a **back** stitch. The method can be used for both starting and finishing.

5. A tiny back stitch
Bring the needle up at A and take it down again close by, at B. Bring it up again at A, and insert it again at B.

Line stitches

Stem stitch

For stems. Stem stitch, as the name implies, is widely used for working plant stems. The stem width can be increased by working extra rows in close parallel lines, but the loop of working thread must be held towards the previous row to ensure the stitches lie together smoothly.

You may work from the *top* or *bottom* of a stem, but the working loop of thread must be held towards any previous row and if possible on the outside of the curve being worked.

FIG 1 shows a stem curving to the left with the loop held temporarily by the left thumb. If a stem curves to the right, it is impossible to hold the loop on this side as the right thumb is holding the needle. By turning the frame from top to bottom the loop can be held by the left thumb as before.

As a *filling stitch.* Stem stitch is a useful filling stitch. It is suitable for larger areas, as in *Apples,* p. 97. It is worked in adjacent rows and can be shaded by graduating the tones of thread, row by row from light to dark. The loop of working thread must be held towards the previous row, and each row must nestle closely against the previous one.

Point to remember

The fabric must be absolutely taut in the frame
when stem stitch is used as a filling stitch.

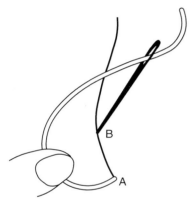

1. Working a stem

The solid line represents the curving stem. Bring up the needle at A and take it down at B while holding the loop of thread to one side with the left thumb.

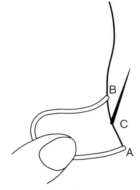

2. *Bring the needle up at C, release the loop and pull the stitch taut to follow the marked stem line.*

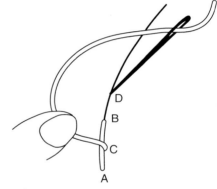

3. *Insert the needle at D and hold the loop once again with your left thumb. Make sure that the distance from B to C is the same as from B to D.*

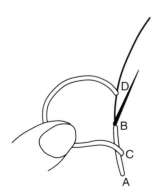

4. *As the needle emerges at B pull the loop taut.*

5. *Campanula*

Design with stems of different widths, to be worked in adjacent rows of stem stitch. Extra rows are added as a stem widens to achieve a natural look.

Split stitch

Split stitch is widely used for outlining in this book. It creates a smooth edge over which subsequent stitches can be worked. It can also be used as a filling stitch, when the ends of adjacent stitches must be staggered, creating a 'brickwork' effect.

Working split stitch is illustrated below, where a leaf edge is shown being outlined in preparation for covering in long & short stitch or satin stitch. The needle splits into the thread of the previous stitch from above. The outline also provides light padding.

Point to remember

When working along a curve, ensure that the stitches follow the line. This is achieved by reinserting the needle on the line of the curve *after* splitting into the previous stitch, as at *F* in FIG 3. In this way a stitch which is naturally straight can be eased round a curve.

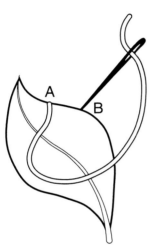

1. Working in split stitch along a curved edge

Bring up the needle at A and take it down at B.

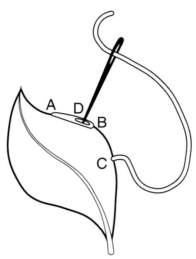

2. Bring the needle up at C and insert it back into the previous stitch at D, splitting the single thread.

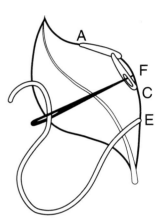

3. Correct the angle of the stitch by inserting the needle on the line, at F, thus easing it onto the curve.

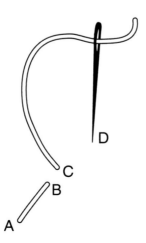

Running stitch

Running stitch is a basic sewing stitch which can be used in embroidery to apply padding materials, see *Apples*, p. 97. It is also used on its own as light padding beneath satin stitch, worked in adjacent rows and at right angles to the stitches above.

1. Running stitch

Bring the needle up at A and pull through the thread. Take the needle down at B and bring it up again at C, a short distance away. Pull the thread gently to form a straight stitch from A to B. Insert the needle at D to make another straight stitch. Repeat as required.

Couching stitch or laid work

Couching is particularly useful for outlining the more prominent features of flowers or insects in embroidery. It has two components: the laid thread and the couching thread (shaded in the diagrams) which secures the laid thread in position. The couching thread is usually thinner than the laid thread.

Follow FIGS 1 to 5. Start by bringing up the thread to be laid at A. Secure its loose end underneath with two small back stitches, using the couching thread. Make sure these stitches lie within the design area, where they will later be hidden by surface stitching.

Space, angle and tension the couching stitches as evenly as possible. This is particularly important when using contrasting colours for the couching and laid threads.

The spacing may need adjustment for sudden changes of angle, as in the edges of the daffodil trumpets, p. 93. At such points work one or two couching stitches closely together to accommodate the change.

To finish see FIG 4.

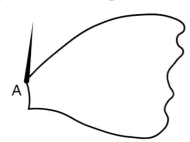

1. Couching a thread on the outline of a butterfly wing

The needle emerging at A carries the thread to be laid.

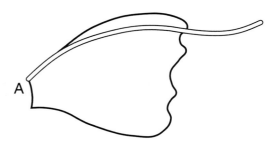

2. The laid thread hangs loosely from A across the working area, leaving a short loose end beneath the fabric. With a single strand of couching thread secure the loose end of the laid thread below with two small back stitches worked one on top of the other.

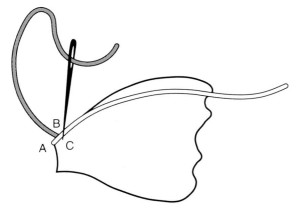

3. The couching thread, in either a matching or contrasting colour, is brought up at B and taken down over the laid thread at C. Be careful not to pierce the laid thread. Choose the angle for your couching stitch and keep to it. Here it is at right angles to the laid thread, but see also Fig. 5.

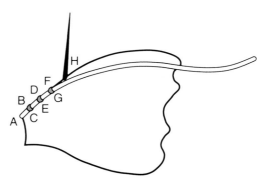

4. The first three couching stitches are worked from B to G and continue from H. When the couching is complete take the laid thread down to the back of the fabric and secure it with two small back stitches, positioned so they will later be covered by stitching.

5. Couching stitches worked diagonally give a smoother finish than the same stitch worked at right angles.

Knotted stitches

French knots

French knots are a valuable method of adding texture in surface embroidery and are particularly useful for representing stamens.

They were used in the daisies and the oilseed rape plant on the *Sampler*, p. 65. In *Poppies*, p. 91, where they were worked in graduated shades over the felt padding of the bud, they add a truly 3-dimensional effect.

French knots can be worked with a single strand. To make larger ones just add more strands or use a thicker thread, e.g. coton perlé no. 5. ***Never*** wrap the thread more than once round the needle.

Poppy bud
To be worked in French knots in shades of green. Darker knots are used for the shadows and the central dividing line.

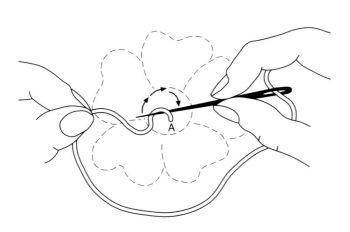

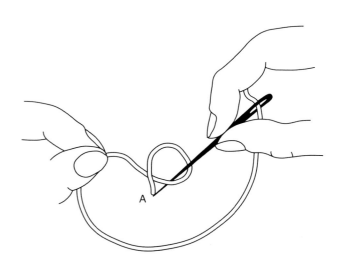

1. Bring up the thread at A. Lay the hoop temporarily on your knee so that both hands are free. Hold the thread between the left thumb and forefinger as illustrated. Bring the needle horizontally from behind with the other hand, and loop the thread over the needle as shown. Rotate the needle clockwise above the fabric, see arrows, and point it down towards A, maintaining the loop around it.

2. Insert the needle into the fabric just next to A, but not through the same hole.

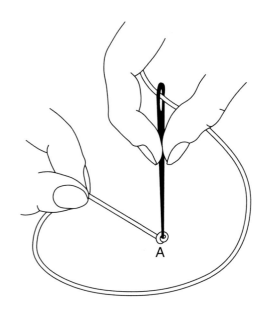

3. With the left hand pull the loop taut to form the knot, remembering that the thickest part of the needle must pass through it. Hold the needle vertically and take it through the fabric while maintaining light tension on the thread with the left hand.

French knots on stalks

French knots on stalks are very effective for working tiny stamens or representing small radiating flowers like the *Thalictrum flower* (below) or the cow parsley in the *Sampler*, p. 65. To add body French knots may be interspersed between the stalks. Radiating knots on stalks must not all emerge from the same spot or a hole may appear in the fabric. They are normally worked with one or two strands of cotton but a thicker thread, e.g. Madeira silk, can be used instead.

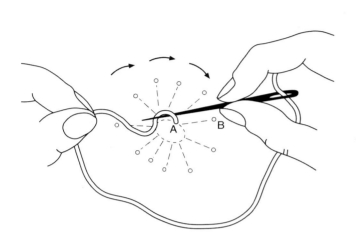 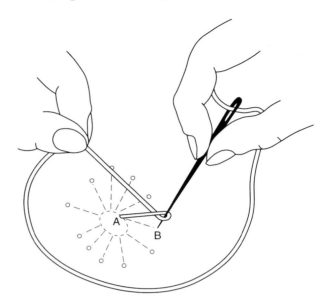

1. Bring up the thread at A and form a loop over the needle as for the ordinary French knot, opposite. Rotate the needle clockwise to complete the loop, see arrows.

2. Insert the needle at B and pull the thread gently with the left hand. Allow the loop to slide down the needle and rest on the surface of the fabric. Take the needle through the fabric at B while maintaining the tension on the thread with the left hand.

 3. Example of flower worked as a ring of French knots on stalks.

THALICTRUM (MEADOW RUE) FLOWER

You will need

Embroidery hoop, 4 in (10 cm). Closely woven linen or satinised cotton, 8 in (20 cm) square. Thread: Anchor stranded cotton.

Embroidery	Colour	Thread No	Stitches
Flower head	pink-magenta	86, 87	French knots on stalks, French knots
Stems	grey-green,	215	stem stitch
'buds'	pink-magenta	*87*	French knots

1. Transfer the outline and mount the fabric.

2. Work the flowers in 2-stranded French knots on stalks, the two side ones in 86 and the middle one in 87.

3. Work the upper stems in single rows of **stem stitch** with one strand of 215, and the lower stem with two adjacent rows. Add 2-stranded French knot 'buds' in 87 where all the stems join.

Bullion knots

This versatile stitch has many uses in embroidery. Bullion knots are very effective as small rose buds, see *Berberis* p. 79, or as thin petals, e.g. *Clover* and the clover in the *Sampler*, p. 65. They can form the raised edges of petals, as for a lilac, or sepals for buds, seed heads and berries. In the centres of larger flowers, like the rhododendron in *Fig. 3* of *Spring*, long bullion knots can represent the filaments of stamens.

This stitch is well worth mastering. For flowers I prefer to use two or more strands of cotton or, better still, two strands of Madeira silk which slides beautifully, but start with a practice run to familiarise yourself with the technique.

To practise bullion knots

1. Mount a piece of tightly-woven fabric, e.g. calico, onto a small hoop. Don't use a loosely-woven fabric or the knot will tend to disappear through it. It is essential that the fabric is mounted *drum-tight* in your hoop to work this stitch effectively.

Use an embroidery needle with a long thin eye.

2. Two strands of cotton or coton perlé no. 5 are fine for practising.

3. Follow the instructions on FIGS 1 to 8 overleaf.

(continued on p. 78)

Clover

Designed and embroidered by the author

Here is a lavish and effective use of bullion knots. See also the example in 'Sampler', p. 65. Embroidery actual size.

You will need

Embroidery hoop, 6 in (15 cm). Closely woven linen or satinised cotton, 10 in (25 cm) square. Vilene padding. Threads: DMC stranded cotton (D), Madeira silk (M).

Embroidery notes

Transfer the outline and mount the fabric, see pp. 67, 106. Stitches and surface effects highlighted in the instructions in **bold** type are explained in detail elsewhere in *Stitches & Techniques*. Use the finished embroidery as a guide to shading.

1. **Pad** the centre of the flower with two oval layers of vilene, the smaller layer first, FIG 1.

2. Work **close fishbone** stitch in 2 strands of green over the padding. This sets the angle for the **bullion knots** to be worked on top and provides shadow in gaps between them, FIG 2.

3. Work 3-stranded **bullion knots** round the perimeter of the padding, continuing the lines of the **close fishbone** stitch. Shade from light at the top to dark at the base in pinks and mauves.

Don't work the knots too evenly: add extra loops to some so that they curve and give a natural look. Add extra knots to the middle to enhance the 3-dimensional effect.

4. Add some **seeding** stitches to soften gaps between knots.

5. Work the bud in pink 1-stranded **bullion knots**, with green ones at the base for the sepals.

6. Work the leaves in **long & short** stitch and the stems in **stem** stitch.

1. Flower centre, guide to padding Apply the smaller layer first.

2. Clover flower
Close fishbone stitch worked over padding, with perimeter bullion knots – more will be added.

Embroidery	Colour	Thread No	Stitches & surface effects
Flower petals	green, pink, mauve	D469, M0613, 0701, 0703, 0801, 0803	padding, close fishbone stitch, bullion knots, seeding stitch
Bud petals	pink, green	*M0613, 0701, D469*	bullion knots
Bud sepals	green	*D469*	bullion knots
Leaves & stem	yellow-green, green	D472, 471, *469*	long & short stitch, stem stitch

The embroidery sections and threads are listed in order of working. Repeat threads are shown in ***bold italics***.

Bullion knots, *continued from p. 76.*

1. *Cut a length of thread, not longer than 16 in (40 cm), and separate the strands before pairing or threading them.*

Don't leave a long end of thread hanging from the needle as this can get caught up in the coil and prevent it sliding smoothly. Bring the needle up at A. Secure the thread below with two tiny straight stitches worked one on top of the other.

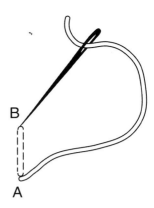

2. *Take the needle down at B, but leave a loop on top. The distance A to B, shown by the broken lines, will be the length of your bullion knot.*

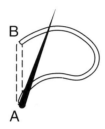

3. *Bring up part of the needle at A. Maintain the loop from A to B as shown, leaving the rest of the thread beneath.*

Grip the eye of the needle below the fabric with the right hand, retaining about a third of its length underneath. Use the other finger tips of the right hand to support the underside of the fabric in the hoop and keep it horizontal.

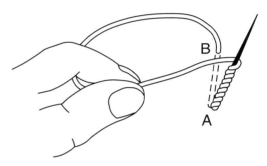

4. *Hold the main loop of thread between thumb and forefinger of the left hand and wind loops anticlockwise round the projecting needle. Ensure the loops lie next to and not on top of each other.*

The number of loops will depend on the length of the bullion knot required; here from A to B. Measure the required length against the projecting needle and add enough turns to match this. Add 3 or 4 extra turns for good measure. Pull up more thread through B if necessary. By adding yet more loops you can create a curved bullion knot.

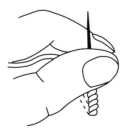

5. *Hold the needle and coil of thread with the thumb and forefinger of the left hand and twist the coil slightly clockwise to loosen it a little. This will allow the eye of the needle to slide easily through the coil.*

Holding the coil with the left hand, grip the tip of the needle with the right thumb and forefinger and draw it right through the coil.

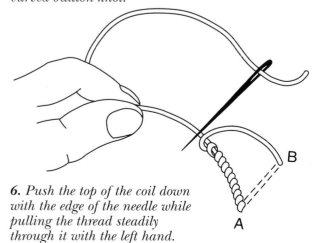

6. *Push the top of the coil down with the edge of the needle while pulling the thread steadily through it with the left hand.*

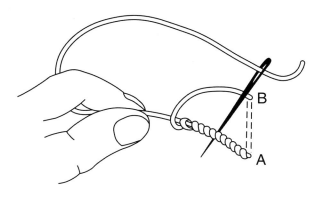

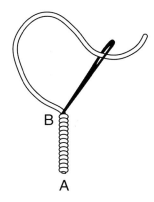

7. *Even out the coil by gently rubbing the side of the needle back and forth along its underside while maintaining a steady tension on the core thread.*

Alternate this process with that from Fig. 6 until the coil lies flat on the fabric.

8. *Reinsert the needle at B and take the thread through ready to start the next knot.*

Points to remember

A common early problem, even after one or two bullion knots have been completed successfully, is that the thread won't slide. This is because the short end of thread becomes a bit ragged and when the next knot is worked the end gets caught in the coil and won't slide free easily. The answer is to keep the short end really short and trim from time to time.

Sometimes when very fine bullion knots are being worked the needle or thread sticks inside the coil. The answer is to give the coil a downwards push with the thumbnail and at the same time lightly pull the central core thread with the other hand.

The finished coil should appear tightly packed and evenly wound over its entire length. It may help left-handed embroiderers to view the diagrams in a mirror.

Bullion knot rose

9. *Bullion knot rose*

a. *Work a triangle of bullion knots.*

b. *Add a ring of bullion knots round the triangle, and anchor each with a couching stitch. The stitches are shown displaced outward for clarity. For a raised effect leave them uncouched and overlapping the inner stitches. To make larger roses add more bullion knots round the outside.*

c. *Complete the rose with a French knot made with several strands of thread, or with a single bead.*

10. *Berberis flowers worked as bullion knot roses.*

Looped stitches

Detached chain stitch

Detached chain stitch can be used to depict small oval flowers like the *Forget-me-not*.

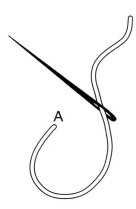

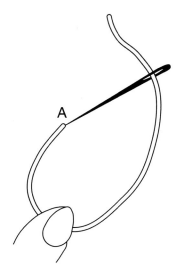

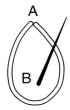

1. *Bring the needle up at A and pull the thread through.*

2. *Reinsert the needle at A, leaving a loop held temporarily with the left thumb.*

3. *Bring part of the needle up at B and release the thumb-hold.*

4. *Pull the needle through and tension the thread, drawing a taut but not tight oval loop up to B.*

Reinsert the needle over the loop at C, drawing the thread through to the back of the fabric.

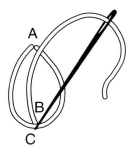

5. *Pull the thread taut to create a small anchoring stitch between B & C. You can now start the next loop.*

Continuous chain stitch

This stitch can be used to embroider a line, particularly for lettering. It can also be used to outline areas for light padding, see p. 98.

Work the initial stages as for detached chain stitch, using FIGS 1 to 3 above; then follow FIGS 1 & 2 here.

1. *Pull the thread right through at B to form a taut but not tight loop between A & B.*
Reinsert the needle at B, leaving another loop held temporarily with the left thumb.

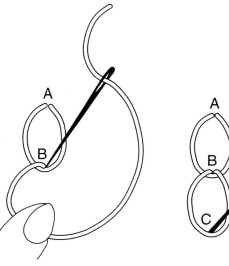

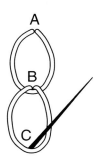

2. *Bring the needle up at C to start another loop. Repeat the whole process to form a line of stitches.*

Forget-me-not

Designed and embroidered by the author

The forget-me-not is one of the very few garden plants in Britain whose open flowers are truly blue, though in bud it is mauve-pink. This project uses detached chain stitch for working tiny petals. Embroidery actual size.

You will need

Embroidery hoop, 6 in (15 cm). Closely woven linen or satinised cotton, 10 in (25 cm) square. Threads: stranded cottons from your collection.

Embroidery notes

Transfer the outline and mount the fabric, see pp. 67, 106. Stitches and effects in **bold** type are explained elsewhere in *Stitches & Techniques*. Use the finished embroidery as a guide to shading.

The flowers. Embroider the round petals in loosely worked **detached chain** stitch and fill them out with a single **straight** stitch, sometimes in a contrasting colour. Work the centres in 2-stranded **French knots**.

The buds. The lower left-hand cluster of buds is also worked in green **detached chain** stitch interspersed with mauve and pink **French knots**. **French knot** buds between flowers are worked with 2, 3, or 4 strands.

Leaves & stems. Work the two smallest leaves in **close fishbone** stitch, adding pale green **stem** stitch veins on the left hand one. Work the large leaves in **satin** stitch from the middle outwards following the directional lines. Next outline the central veins in cream yellow **stem** stitch. Small **straight** stitches in a contrasting colour can be added on top of the **satin** stitches to suggest side veins. Edge parts of some leaves in **stem** stitch with one strand of dark green thread to create shadow. Work the stems in **stem** stitch.

Embroidery	Colour	Stitches & surface effects
Open flower petals	blue, mauve-pink	detached chain stitch, straight stitch
Flower centres	blue, mauve-pink	French knots
Buds	green, mauve, pink	French knots, detached chain stitch
Small leaves	green, light green	close fishbone stitch
Large leaves	green, dark green	satin stitch
Central veins	cream-yellow	stem stitch
Side veins	dark green	straight stitch
Leaf edges	dark green	stem stitch
Stems	green	stem stitch

The embroidery sections and colours are listed in order of working.

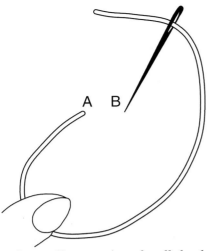

Fly stitch

Fly stitch is like an open detached chain stitch, also known as *open loop stitch*. It is useful for defining the edges and tips of tiny petals.

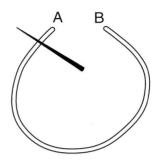

1. Bring the needle up at A and pull the thread through. Reinsert the needle at B, leaving a loop held temporarily with the left thumb.

2. Bring the needle up at C, forming a triangle with A & B.

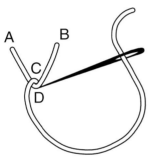

4. The completed fly stitch.

3. Release the thumb-hold and pull the thread taut to produce the V shape of the fly stitch. Insert the needle over the thread at D to form a couching stitch which will hold the V in position.

5. Examples of fly stitch

a. Forming the petals of a tiny flower, with a French knot for the centre and stem stitch for the stalk.

b. Forming a bud together with detached chain stitch, and stem stitch for the stalk. The open spaces can be filled with straight stitches.

Fishbone stitches

Fishbone stitch has open and close forms, both of which are V-shaped with a central divide. Both are widely used in this book.

Open fishbone stitch

The V-shape of the open fishbone stitch is particularly suitable for depicting fine stems and leaves, including sprigs of heather and yarrow, see the *Sampler*, p. 65 and *Heather* exercise below.

Points to remember

When transferring pattern outlines with areas to be worked in open fishbone stitch, e.g. *Heather* below, transfer *only* the central line. The V-shapes will be formed by the stitches themselves.

Beginners may wonder why the angles of their V-shapes start to straighten out. Maintaining this angle depends on the length of the central straight stitch, *A* to *B* and *B* to *E*, FIG 3. If these straight stitches become too short the accompanying V-shape will lose its characteristic angle. The answer is to keep the length of the central stitch the same throughout.

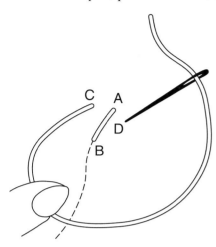

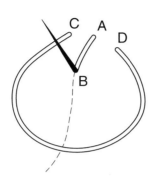

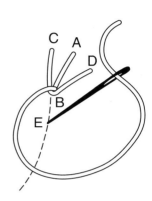

1. Start by working a straight stitch from A to B. The broken line shows the direction of working. Bring the needle up again at C. Hold the thread in a loop with the left thumb and take the needle down at D.

2. Bring the needle up at B once more, release the loop and gently draw the thread taut to form the V-shaped stitch.

3. Insert the needle over the thread at E to anchor the V-shaped stitch firmly in position, and to start the next stitch.

Repeat 1 to 3 to form a line of V-shaped stitches.

HEATHER

Here is a design for practising open fishbone stitch.

Trace the stems, flowers and buds only. ***Don't*** trace the V-shaped leaves, which will be added naturally as you work the main stem in **open fishbone** stitch. Using single strands of cotton, work the flowers and buds in purple, pink and magenta **detached chain** stitch, and the short flower stem in **stem** stitch.

Threads: stranded cottons from your collection.

Embroidery	Colour	Stitches
Main stem & leaves	green	open fishbone stitch
Flowers, buds	purple, pink	detached chain stitch
Flower stem	green	stem stitch

Close fishbone stitch

This too is a V-shaped stitch and is worked in a similar way to open fishbone stitch, but very close together. It is suitable for small leaves, see clover in the *Sampler*, and for petals, as in *Bluebells* opposite. It is usually worked over a split stitch outline which provides slight padding.

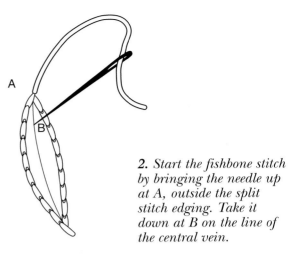

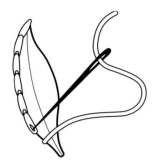

1. Preparing the edge

Outline the leaf in split stitch to form a firm edge. The fishbone stitches will be worked over this edge, giving a neat and slightly padded look.

2. Start the fishbone stitch by bringing the needle up at A, outside the split stitch edging. Take it down at B on the line of the central vein.

3. Bring the needle up at C, slightly below and to the left of A. Holding the thread in a loop with the left thumb, insert the needle at D, slightly below and to the right of A.

4. Bring the needle up again at B. Release the thumb-hold and gently pull taut the narrow V-shaped stitch. Reinsert the needle over the thread at E, a short way from B, to secure the first stitch and start the next. Repeat Figs 1 to 4 to cover the rest of the leaf.

5. *The fully covered leaf*

As with open fishbone stitch, the length of the central straight stitch (B to E, Fig. 4) controls the V-angle of the next stitch. The shorter the straight stitch the flatter the V-angle.

Note that below the three central stitches marked with a dot are slightly shorter unmarked ones. The shorter stitches allow the V-angles to flatten a little, but if they were much shorter the angles would flatten almost completely and spoil the overall effect.

Designed and embroidered by the author.

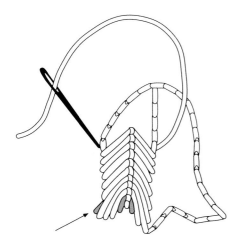

6. Working a bluebell flower

The edges and central dividing line were outlined in split stitch. On the left half, close fishbone stitch is being worked over the outline from the lower edge upwards. A difficult shape can be filled by making some stitches shorter than others, or by adding extra straight or stem stitches (shown shaded).

Once the lower edge has been filled with stitches the angle will tend to flatten out naturally. Don't allow the stitches to become too flat, however. If necessary lengthen the centre stitch a little to avoid it.

Bluebell flowers worked in close fishbone stitch with stranded cottons on linen union. Mauves and blues can be mixed and matched but one side of each bell should be kept lighter. Slightly enlarged detail.

Filling stitches

Long and short stitch

Long & short stitch is a versatile filling stitch used extensively in this book for both leaves and flowers. It is particularly effective and pleasing to the eye when used for shading and blending of colour tones. It does however require practice!

FIGS 1 to 7 have been devised as a practice run, in two stages. FIGS 1 to 4 teach the basics of the stitch. Figs 5 to 7 show the stitch applied to a simple petal shape. FIG 8 is an irregular leaf.

Practice on a spare piece of fabric before tackling a project. Gather together 3 lengths of crewel wool in light, medium and dark tones of one colour. Stretch the fabric on a small hoop frame and draw a line to work along.

continued overleaf

Long & short stitch, *continued*

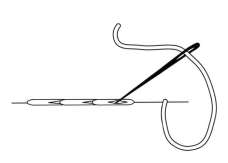 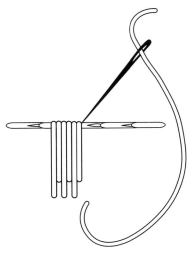 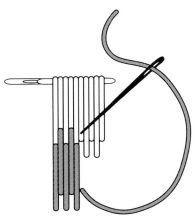

1. Making the edge in split stitch

Use a single strand of the lightest shade of wool to work a line in split stitch. Make each stitch $1/4$ in (6 mm) long. The split stitch provides a firm padded edge to work over.

2. Working the first row in long & short stitch

Use the lightest tone again to work a row of adjacent long & short stitches, in alternate $1/4$ in (6 mm) and $1/3$ in (8 mm) lengths. Keep the short stitches at about $3/4$ of the length of the long stitches. These alternating lengths should produce a softly undulating line, not a straight one.

3. Working the second row

Work a row of long stitches **only** in mid tone, splitting down into the ends of the light-toned stitches.

All stitches in the second and following rows are the same length, despite their staggered look. They simply dovetail into the alternating lengths of the first row.

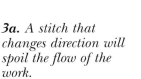

3a. A stitch that changes direction will spoil the flow of the work.

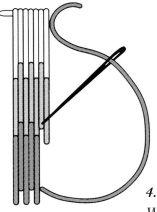

4. Working the third row

Work in a darker tone, splitting down into the previous mid-toned stitches.

Try to achieve the same length of stitch as in the second row, bearing in mind that each subsequent row partially obscures the true length of the previous row.

Points to remember

In the course of work you will have to fill awkward shapes, but the following guidelines will help you maintain a smooth blend of stitches.

1. Long & short stitch is intended to produce a soft line and blending tones, not straight edges or abrupt changes, so no two adjacent stitches should ever finish at exactly the same level. If they do they will create a hardness which will be almost impossible to disguise.

2. Avoid abrupt changes of angle. Fig 3a gives an example of such a mistake.

3. Avoid abrupt changes of tone.

4. A frequent mistake is that stitches get shorter and shorter as work progresses. This can easily occur when 3 or 4 tones of thread need to be fitted into a limited space. The answer is to maintain the initial length of stitch, but split further into the preceding row of stitches with each subsequent row.

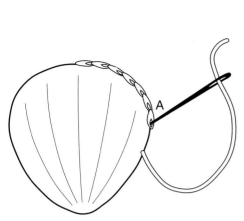 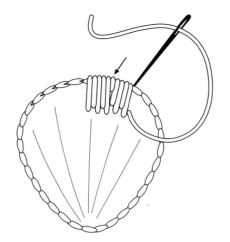 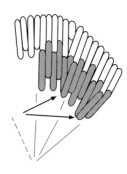

5. Outlining a simple petal

Draw the petal outline with a transfer pencil: make the width and length each about 1 in (25 mm).

Draw in the directional guide lines. The stitches are normally worked from the outer edge to the base – from a wide space into a narrower one.

Secure the thread with a waste knot, then outline the petal in ¼ in (6 mm) split stitches in a light tone.

6. Working the first row in long & short stitch

*Work from the **centre top to the right** with the lightest shade of thread, as in Fig. 2. To adjust for the tapering space between the guide lines add a small stitch at the edge, shown by the arrow. This stitch will subtly alter the direction of subsequent stitches. This can only be done on the first row, where it is inconspicuous. Return to the centre and work the row **to the left**, adding extra small stitches as required.*

7. Working the second row

Start from the centre once again in a darker tone. This row appears to be long & short, but is all the same length. See also Fig. 3.

To adjust to the narrowing space, work two long stitches into the same point at intervals, as shown by the arrows. When working the third row, treat the merged stitches as one and split back into it.

Darken the tone row by row towards the centre.

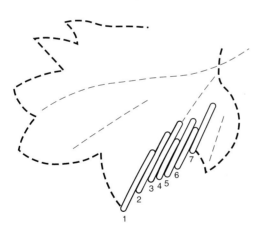

8. Working a shape with an irregular outline
Long & short stitch cannot be worked here in the usual regular pattern.

a. Stitches 1-3 are long ones of almost equal length. They will produce the staggered edge required on the inside as well as the leaf edge.

Avoid more than three adjacent long stitches in such a position: they will create a hard line, difficult to disguise in following rows.

b. For **stitches 3-7**, where the edge is straighter, work long & short stitch in the usual manner.

c. Continue the second and third rows of long & short stitch, see Figs 3, 4 & 7 above.

Points to remember

5. When mixing stitches in silk with stitches in crewel wool, work the silk before the wool wherever possible as the threads will blend better.

6. The general rule for direction is to work from the edge inwards. For leaves follow the angles of the side veins towards the central vein. For petals work from the edge to the base along the radial lines shown in FIGS 5 to 7, which are also its natural lines.

However, autumnal leaves with small serrated edges, e.g. of roses or blackberries, are best worked from the central vein outwards. **Split** stitch the central vein. Work the first row of long & short stitch over the **split** stitched line, and continue in the direction of the secondary veins.

7. Long & short stitch automatically becomes **satin** stitch when worked in a single row along a narrowing area, as illustrated in *Poppies, Daffodils* and *Apples*.

Satin stitch

Satin stitch is a useful filling stitch for buds, small flowers, berries, and narrow shapes such as the oats in the *Sampler*, p. 65. It looks best in very closely worked parallel lines without visible space between them. Sudden changes in angle, particularly in a single stitch, will spoil its smooth texture and characteristic sheen. This stitch requires practice and patience.

Very long stitches, which need anchoring, and very short ones, which break the satin effect, are undesirable in satin stitch, so the layout of stitches must be considered before starting. If the subject is a flower (FIG 1), angle the stitches towards the centre but also try to vary the angle from petal to petal, to distinguish one from another. Further variety can be achieved by contrasting the tones or varying the shades of adjacent petals.

1. Working a simple flower in satin stitch (enlarged)
Shows the outlining stitches and directional lines.

First outline the petals in split stitch to form a firm edge. Don't outline the joins between the petals. Mark the directional lines on the fabric. Each petal is worked in two halves, from middle to tip, then from middle to flower centre.

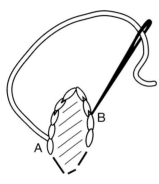

2. The first satin stitch

Start from the middle of the petal and work outwards. Bring the needle up at A and take it down at B, outside the split stitch edging. Angle the slanting stitches along the pencilled guide lines.

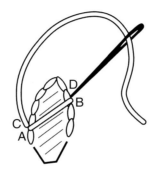

3. The second satin stitch

Bring the needle up at C and take it down at D. Continue until you cover the tip of the petal.

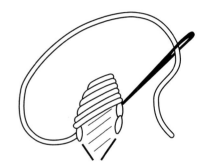

4. The lower half of the petal

Return from the tip to the middle of the petal through the backs of the stitches and fill the lower half.

Points to remember

You may find the angle of stitches tends to flatten out. The answer is to work the stitches at the upper (right hand) edge close together, FIG 3, but leave a little space between them at the lower edge. This will tilt the angle slightly and usually corrects the problem. Any adjustment in angle must be done very gradually.

For a really rounded look the satin stitch can first be lightly padded, see p. 98.

Avoid gaps between stitches where the fabric could show through. More stitches will be required in practice than appear in the diagrams.

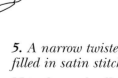

5. A narrow twisted leaf filled in satin stitch

Note the gradually changing angle of stitching. On the tight inner curve, shown by the arrow, stitches are worked close together. On the wider outside curve opposite, more space is left between the same stitches to match the greater width.

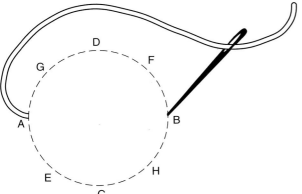

Whipped spider web stitch

This stitch can be used to depict the centres of open roses, the centres of *Poppies* (p. 91), and the tops of seed heads, as in the *Sampler*. In nature the top of a ripening poppy seed-head looks almost identical to an embroidered whipped spider web stitch. This stitch resembles a spoked wheel, with the thread tightly wound ('whipped') round the radial stitches, starting from the centre. Loosen tension slightly as you work towards the edge. Use a single strand of thread.

1. Forming the 'spokes'

Work in the alphabetical order of the letters. Bring the needle up at A and take it down at B on the opposite edge. Repeat for C to D, E to F and G to H to create the 'spokes'.

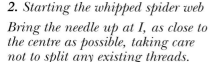
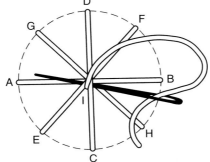
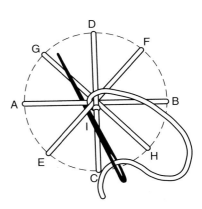

2. Starting the whipped spider web

Bring the needle up at I, as close to the centre as possible, taking care not to split any existing threads.

3. Working the 'whipping' stitch

Bring the thread through at I and change to a fine tapestry needle, or reverse the crewel needle and use the eye end to embroider.

    Work back over the previous thread CD, then under it and under the next, EF, making sure the needle doesn't pierce either the fabric or the threads. Bring the thread up carefully between E & A and repeat the process clockwise round the centre, see Fig. 4.

4. Continuing round the centre

Take the needle back over thread EF and slide it forward under EF & AB. Repeat for AB & GH, etc, working tightly packed stitches round the centre.

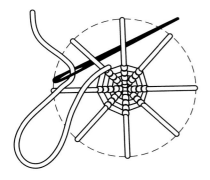

5. Centre of the whipped spider web

Loosen the tension a little as you leave the centre. You can fill the web with stitches or leave the tips of the 'spokes' exposed.

To finish transfer the thread to the back of the fabric with a crewel needle. Secure the end with two small straight stitches worked one on top of the other.

Poppies

Designed by the author, embroidered by Moira Postans

Poppies are a highlight of the garden in early summer. This striking oriental poppy will exercise your shading skills: in split stitch for the petals and long & short stitch for the leaves. It also illustrates how split stitch, a line stitch, can be used for filling. Embroidery reduced size.

You will need

Embroidery hoop, 12 in (30 cm). Cream linen union, 16 in (40 cm) square. Black seed beads. Vilene and white felt padding. Threads: Appleton crewel wool (A), Madeira silk (M).

Embroidery	Colour	Thread No	Stitches & effects
Flower petals	cream, orange, flamingo, coral	M0112, 0114, A623, 625, 866	split stitch, padding
base streaks	purple	A104, 106	
Flower centre & stamens	mauve, purple	M0801, 0803, *A106*	straight, stem stitches, French knots, beading
Opening bud	orange, flamingo, coral	*M0114, A623, 625, 866*	French knots
Seed head & closed bud	pastel, grass green early English green	A872, 251a, 253, 254, 548	split stitch, padding, long & short stitch, beading, French knot
Stems, leaves	green, grass green, early English green	M1409(stems), *A251a*, 543, 545, 547, *548*	split, stem, straight, long & short, satin stitches

The embroidery sections and threads are listed in order of working. Repeat threads are shown in ***bold italics***.

Embroidery notes

Transfer the outline and mount the fabric, see pp. 67, 111. Stitches and surface effects highlighted in **bold** type are explained in detail elsewhere in ***Stitches & Techniques***. Work in single strands throughout unless stated otherwise. Use the finished embroidery as a guide to shading.

1. Outline the petals (A623), seed head and buds (A251a), and leaves (A543) in **split** stitch.

2. Pad the closed bud and seed head with two layers of felt, and the flower centre with two layers of vilene. **Pad** the sepals of the opening bud with a single layer of vilene. Add guide lines for the seed head over the padding.

Flowers

3. Shade the petals in adjacent rows of **split** stitch. Work from the edge to the base following the directional lines. Use double-stranded silk for the highlights and wool for the darker streaks and shadows. Add the purple streaks at the base.

4. Create the oval flower centre with **straight** stitches in mauve silks, working from the edge in. Work the stamens in purple (A106) **straight** or **stem** stitch, tipped with 2-stranded **French knots** in mauve silk or black seed **beads**.

Opening bud

5. Work the petal and sepals with single-stranded **French knots** in orange, flamingo and coral. Add a few 2-stranded **French knots** to the upper part in orange for highlights.

Seed head & closed bud

6. Work the seed head in **long & short** stitch from the base up. Add 5 radiating rows of **beads** at the top. Fill the bud in **French knots** in the greens and pastels listed, shading to enhance the 3-dimensional effect.

Stems & leaves

7. Embroider the stems in adjacent rows of **stem** stitch shading from light to dark, adding highlights in silk M1409. Use the same silk in small **straight** stitches for hairs on the stems.

8. Work the leaves in **long & short** stitch following the directional lines. Narrow sections can be embroidered in **satin** stitch. Work the central veins, but only on upper leaves, in grass green (A251a) **stem** stitch.

91

Seeding stitch

Seeding, sometimes called 'speckling', is a simple but effective way of adding texture. Its effect is similar to fine brush strokes on a painting. Worked closely and at random angles, it can be used for the rough texture of branches, as for *Apples*, p. 97. where it adds depth beneath the French and bullion knots. When more open and regular, it can portray softly-edged flowers like the furry catkin, see *Daffodils* opposite.

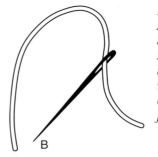

1. Bring the needle up at A and take it down at B. Seeding stitches are very short and of similar length: about $^1/_{16}$ in (1.5 mm) for a single strand of cotton, or $^1/_8$ in (3 mm) for crewel wool.

2. In this cluster the stitches were worked at different angles but quite close to each other. The placing of stitches is important for the correct effect, which appears random yet requires forethought.

Daffodils & pussy willow

Designed and worked by the author

This project will delight experienced embroiderers. Long & short stitch and closely-worked adjacent rows of stem stitch are used to great effect for shading the petals and trumpets, and the trumpets' raised edges are created with a couched thread.

For the pussy willow buds, close fishbone and satin stitches worked over padding create a smoothly raised effect. Seeding stitches, French knots, and French knots on stalks, worked over a core of padding, create the delicate effect of the catkins.

Follow the table for order of working and stitches & effects. Outline, p. 108. Embroidery reduced size.

You will need

Embroidery hoop, 10 in (25 cm). White closely woven linen, 14 in (35 cm). Vilene padding. Threads: Anchor stranded cotton, DMC coton perlé No 5 (CP).

Embroidery	Colour	Thread No	Stitches & effects
Flower petals	yellow	288-290	split stitch, padding,
petal shadows	yellow-green	278, 280	long & short, satin stitches
trumpets	yellow, orange-brown	**288-290**, 298, 305, 302, 307, 308	stem stitch
trumpet edges	yellow	CP445	couching
sheaths	brown	390, 392, 393	split stitch, padding, long & short satin, stem stitches
stems & leaves	green	253-255, 267	stem, split, long & short, satin stitch
Willow branches	olive-green, brown	279, **280**, 281, 889	stem stitch
buds	grey, orange, brown, olive-green	847-849, 363, 365, **889, 279**	split stitch, padding, close fishbone, satin, straight stitches
catkins	yellow, green	*as petals & leaves*	padding, seeding, straight stitches, French knots & Fr. knots on stalks

The embroidery sections and threads are listed in order of working. Repeat threads are shown in **bold italics**.

Straight stitch

A straight stitch is worked in the same way as a seeding stitch, but is longer. It is useful for working thin stamens in the centres of flowers, for contrasting streaks in the centres of pansies, and for side veins on small leaves. Straight stitches, together with fly stitches, can be added to open fishbone stitch in sprigs of heather to give extra body, see the *Sampler*.

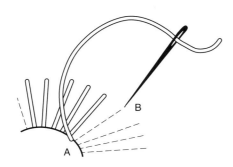

1. Straight stitch for a daisy

Bring the needle up at A and take it down at B along the broken line. Work round the head, but not too evenly or the flower will look unnatural.

2. Straight stitch for a pansy

Mark the dark streaks in straight stitch in the centre of light-coloured pansies and other flowers.

MICHAELMAS DAISIES

*Small thin petals, such as those of the Michaelmas daisy, can be a perfect subject for straight stitch. Work the petals in mauves and purples. Work the ring round the centre in deep yellow **detached chain** stitch and fill the centre with **seeding** stitch or **French knots** in lighter yellow. You could embroider the leaves in **satin** stitch, the sepals in **detached chain** stitch and the **stems** in stem stitch in shades of green.*

The finished embroidery would make an attractive card to mark a special occasion.

Surface effects

Beading

Beads offer a simple and effective way of adding texture and lustre to surface embroidery. They are particularly good for certain soft fruit berries, such as blackberries and raspberries, as well as stamen tips and flower centres. Beading needles, or needles with eyes narrow enough to pass through the beads, are essential. Use a quality dressmaking thread in a matching colour to apply the beads. Alternatively you can use one strand of embroidery cotton, rubbed with beeswax to strengthen it and stitched twice through the bead.

The beads can be stitched on individually: FIG 1 and *Blackberries* (opposite) or in rows: FIGS 2 & 3 and *Poppies*, p. 91.

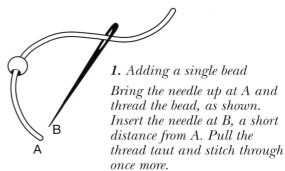

1. Adding a single bead

Bring the needle up at A and thread the bead, as shown. Insert the needle at B, a short distance from A. Pull the thread taut and stitch through once more.

Secure the ends of thread with two tiny back stitches, or with two straight stitches worked one on top of the other. This method is used to add a single bead, or beads clustered among French knots.

94

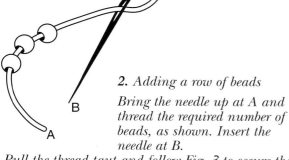

2. *Adding a row of beads*

Bring the needle up at A and thread the required number of beads, as shown. Insert the needle at B.

Pull the thread taut and follow Fig. 3 to secure the beads. The distance AB should equal the total length of all the beads to be used when lined up close together.

Blackberries. Clusters of beads were applied one by one and interspersed with French knots. Enlarged detail.

3. *Anchoring a row of beads*

In this example stitch AB holds three beads. Work couching stitches between each, bringing the needle up between beads 1 & 2 on one side of the row.

Take it over the central thread and reinsert it on the other side close by. This tiny stitch secures the thread between beads 1 and 2. Work a similar couching stitch between beads 2 & 3.

Padding

Padding gives an extra dimension by adding depth and perspective. Areas to pad are those which need to look prominent – to be 'brought forward' – and which are focal points of the design.

The main method used here is to apply layers of 1/16 in (1.6 mm) synthetic stiffening material over areas to be raised. Vilene is a good choice for areas requiring a defined edge, such as petals and leaves. Felt, and its synthetic equivalent Thermalan, are suitable for padding softly rounded shapes, such as poppy seed heads, buds and crab apples. Felt will shrink when wet, but vilene and thermalan will not.

It is easier to tension stitches over vilene, especially over more than one layer, than over felt or thermalan. Other methods use polyester wadding, running stitches, and split stitch or chain stitch edging, see *Alternative methods* below.

1. Outline the edges of shapes to be padded in **split** stitch. This encloses the padding and provides a firm edge to work the filling stitches over.

Areas to be padded are shown unshaded. Shaded areas represent gaps in the padding, as in FIGS 1, 2 & 3, and should *not* be padded.

The gaps are important. Small gaps are left between adjacent sections of padding (FIG 1). Without them, areas will merge instead of being well defined. They create depth by increasing the impression of overlap, defining edges and emphasising separate parts of a plant.

The gap, shown shaded, is always taken out of the section being overlapped. The padded area decreases as the pattern recedes from the eye.

In padded leaves always leave a gap for the central vein, FIG 2.

2. Photocopy the pattern outline and cut out each shape needing padding. To avoid mixing up cut pieces of padding, it is best to cut and apply one before cutting the next.

3. For a single layer place the cut-out shape over the vilene and cut the vilene fractionally smaller than the pattern. The cut shape should fit snugly into the area to be padded.

Attach the padding to the fabric with small overcast stitches round the edges, FIG 4, using white cotton sewing thread.

4. More than one layer is needed for shapes like apples, berries and daisy centres. Apply the smallest layer first, FIG 3. Cut the second and further layers slightly wider than the pattern to allow for the bulge formed by the lower layer.

5. Secure larger areas in the middle with rows of temporary **running** stitches, in addition to the permanent stitches at the edges, see *Apples* opposite. Remove the temporary stitches as the work proceeds.

6. Trace the side veins or directional lines on the padding with a sharp transfer pencil before working **long & short, satin,** or other filling stitches over it.

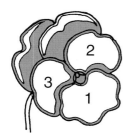

1. Padding a flower

*Work the bold outlines round each unshaded petal area in split stitch. Leave **shaded** areas **unpadded**.*

*Cut out the padding for petal 1. It must fit just inside the outlined petal. Cut the gaps (shown shaded) out of petals 2 & 3 lying behind, **not** from petal 1. Secure the padding (Fig. 4) and mark the directional lines on it. Cut out the next shape and secure it in the same way.*

3. Padding a small apple in two layers

Outline the apple in split stitch. Cut out and secure the smaller layer, which is always applied first. It is shown here unshaded and is not outlined in split stitch.

Cut out and secure the second layer, shown unshaded, on top of the first. Make sure it fits within the split stitched outline, and secure it.

2. Padding a leaf

The tapering central vein requires a gap in the padding. Work the bold outlines round each half of the leaf in split stitch. Cut the padding to fit within the outlines, and secure both pieces (Fig. 4).

Mark the side veins on the padding as a directional guide for the filling stitches to be worked over the padding.

4. Securing a section of padding

Hold it to the fabric with a pin. Starting with the outer edge, secure it all round with overcast stitches.

A larger area of padding will also need rows of temporary running stitches to secure it in the middle, see 'Apples' opposite.

Apples - work in progress
Designed and worked by the author.
The exposed padding reveals overcast stitches worked over the split stitch outline, and temporary running stitches further in. Both help to secure the padding. Working threads not in use are kept together on top of the fabric. A ring of acid-free paper protects against marking, see p. 68. The skeins displayed separately appear in order of shading. Outline on p. 107. Embroidery reduced size.

Padding - alternative methods

Loose polyester wadding

This method is particularly suitable for small berries, such as sorbus, and can be used as an alternative to vilene, e.g. for holly.

Padding a small berry

1. To start outline the edge in **split** stitch, Fig 1.

2. Place a tiny ball of wadding inside the outline and secure it with a circle of small loose **straight** stitches.

3. Work a first layer of **satin** stitch over the wadding as a light padding in a single strand of silk. Reduce bulk on the underside by following the numbered order of stitches in Fig 2.

4. Work a second layer of **satin** stitch across the first, following the numbered order of Fig 3 in the usual way.

Cotoneaster berries
Small berries are suitable for padding with loose polyester wadding.

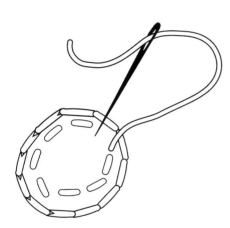

1. *Securing the wadding*

Outline the shape in split stitch in the chosen colour. Secure the wadding with a circle of small loosely-worked straight stitches. More may be applied to the centre of the padding but they should be very loosely worked.

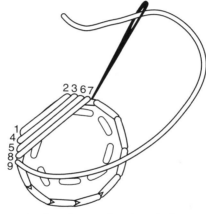

2. *The first layer of satin stitch as a light padding*

Work a first layer of satin stitch over the wadding, but bring the needle up next to the end of the last stitch worked and follow the numbered order to reduce bulk on the underside. Don't use the same pinhole twice.

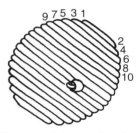

3. *The second layer of satin stitch*

Work the second layer of satin stitch across the first. Follow the numbered order, covering both the top and underside of the fabric in the usual way. Tightly attach a single bead or French knot. This creates a dip, adding a more natural look.

Light padding with stitches

A **split** stitch outline will create a slightly raised or padded edge, adding an illusion of depth and giving a general clarity to the work.

An initial **chain** stitch outline can be a useful alternative since it gives greater width and bulk to the padded outline, but it doesn't provide such a smooth clear edge to work over. This can be solved by first working a **split** stitch edge then, just inside it, a **chain** stitch outline.

Underlying **running** or **seeding** stitches can be used to raise areas where fuller padding with material is unnecessary. Running stitches are best beneath line stitches such as **stem** stitch, and should be worked at *right* angles to them. Seeding stitches, worked at random, are best beneath **satin** stitch and give it a rounded look.

Embroidered picots

Embroidered picots are derived from traditional stump work or raised embroidery. A picot's triangular shape is excellent for creating raised sepals with a 3-dimensional effect. It is used for strawberries, blackberries and other fruit, see detail of *Blackberries* pp. 95, 101.

1. *Outlining the picot*

Decide the size of the triangular picot and place a pin at the apex.

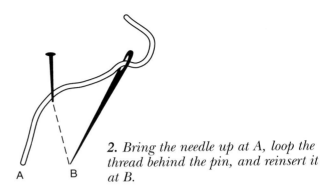

2. *Bring the needle up at A, loop the thread behind the pin, and reinsert it at B.*

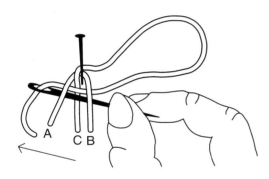

3. *Weaving the picot*

Bring the needle up at C, nearer to B than A, and take the thread round the pin again. To avoid piercing the threads, reverse the needle so the eye becomes the 'point' and start weaving: under B, over C and under A. Pull the thread right through.

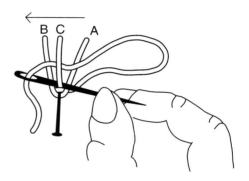

4. *Turn the hoop round 180 degrees. Weave back, with the needle still reversed: over A, under C and over B. Tension the weaver thread, packing it tightly against the pin to form a pointed end for the picot. Packing the weaving will be easier if the pin is flattened to the fabric using the left forefinger from below.*

Continue weaving, turning the frame after each row and tensioning the thread to obtain a tightly-woven picot.

5. *A completed picot*

Remove the pin and secure the thread end with a tiny back stitch.

Once the pin is removed the picot should only be attached to the fabric at A, B & C. The weaving should be packed closely together and the picot should have a good triangular shape.

Banksia rose stitch

This stitch is derived from traditional stump work and makes an effective small rose or cone. It consists of three central loop stitches surrounded by loosely-worked stem stitches of gradually diminishing height.

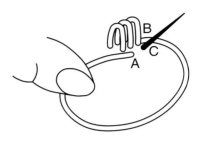

1. Make three closely-worked loop stitches, marked 1 to 3, to form the centre of the rose stitch.

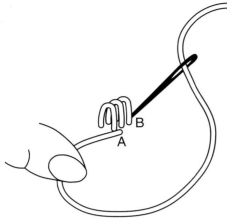

2. Making loop 4 as a loose stem stitch

Bring up the needle close to loop 2, at A. Pull the thread through without distorting loop 3. Hold loop 4 temporarily to one side with the left thumb and insert the needle to the rear of loop 3, at B.

3. Continue to hold loop 4 and bring up the point of the needle at C next to loop 3. At this point it becomes a loosely-worked stem stitch.

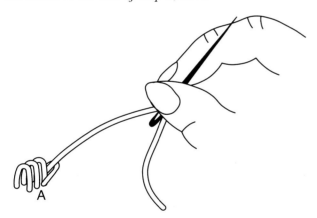

4. Release the thumb-hold and pull loop 4 gently up to the same height as loops 1 to 3. This completes loop 4.

Continue working clockwise around loops 1 to 3 in loose stem stitch, holding each new loop temporarily aside as in Figs 2 & 3, and turning the hoop after each stitch.

Gradually reduce the height of the stitches so that the outer row is almost flush with the surface of the fabric.

5. The finished banksia rose stitch seen from above. The rings of overlapping loose stem stitches enclose the centre of loop stitches.

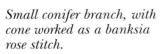

Small conifer branch, with cone worked as a banksia rose stitch.

100

1. Starting the calico slip

Mount a piece of calico in a 4 in (10 cm) hoop. Draw a round or oval outline suitable for a berry onto it, and an outer (broken) line, $^1/_4$ in (6 mm) away.

Sew the beads randomly onto the calico. Some gaps will remain between them.

Calico slip

This surface effect consists of a small piece of calico covered with beading or stitches. It is completed *separately*, then attached to the embroidery and stuffed with a little sheep's wool or polyester wadding. It is very effective for making berries such as blackberries.

2. Filling the gaps and completing the slip

Fill spaces between the beads with 4-stranded French knots in a colour matching the beads.

Cut out the completed slip along the broken line.

Blackberries made with calico slips. Enlarged detail.

3. Attaching the completed slip to the embroidery

Secure the slip round two thirds of its edge with 2-stranded French knots, tucking the cut edge under as you go. The unattached edge of the slip forms a 'pocket' over the fabric.

4. Stuffing the slip

Gently push a little sheep's wool into the 'pocket' with a pair of blunt-ended scissors or tweezers. Sew up the opening with French knots.

Twisted cord

A twisted cord is satisfying to make – simple in construction yet effective in use. It makes an interesting 3-dimensional plant stem, a raised border or lettering, and is secured with couching stitches. Coton perlé or stranded cottons are suitable threads.

For a thicker cord use more thread.

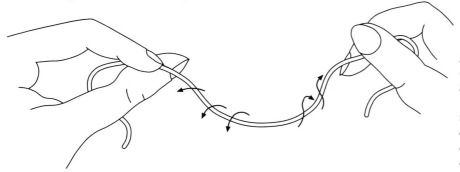

1. Making a twisted cord for a stem
Cut your thread to about three times the final length of cord required. Take each end between thumb and index finger and twist the thread in opposite directions, as shown by the arrows. You can work alone or ask a friend to twist from one end.

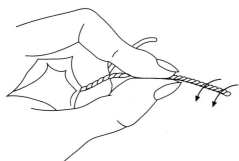

2. To obtain as tight a twist as possible trap the end of the twisted thread between the middle and fourth fingers. This will secure the twist so you can move your thumb and index finger to a new position. As you continue twisting, tension the thread between your hands, otherwise it will start to twist on itself.

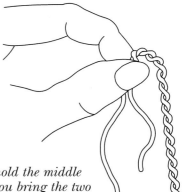

3. Get a friend to hold the middle temporarily while you bring the two ends together, holding them firmly between thumb and index finger.

Once the middle is released, a twisted cord will form automatically. You will find the cord is tighter at the closed end. Continue to hold the open end and even out the cord by running it between the thumb and index finger of your free hand. Tie a knot at the open end to prevent the cord unravelling.

4. Adding the twisted cord to a marigold seed head

Make a small hole in the fabric at X where the lower end of the stem will lie, using a large needle or stiletto. The closed end of the cord will be the top end of the stem. Thread the closed end through a needle and bring it up through the hole. Attach it in position on the embroidery edge with a small stitch, using a single strand in a matching colour.

Lay the cord along the line of the stem and secure it with couching stitches. First bring the needle up at A and take it down at B, then up again at C and down at D, and so on. Secure the cord under the fabric with an invisible back stitch and cut off any excess cord.

Pattern outlines

Outlines for Honeysuckle, Butterfly, Blackberries, Autumn bouquet, Christmas, Thalictrum flower, Heather and Michaelmas daisies appear with their projects, which are listed in the Contents, p. 5.

Winter p. 11

Spring p. 23

Viola p. 28

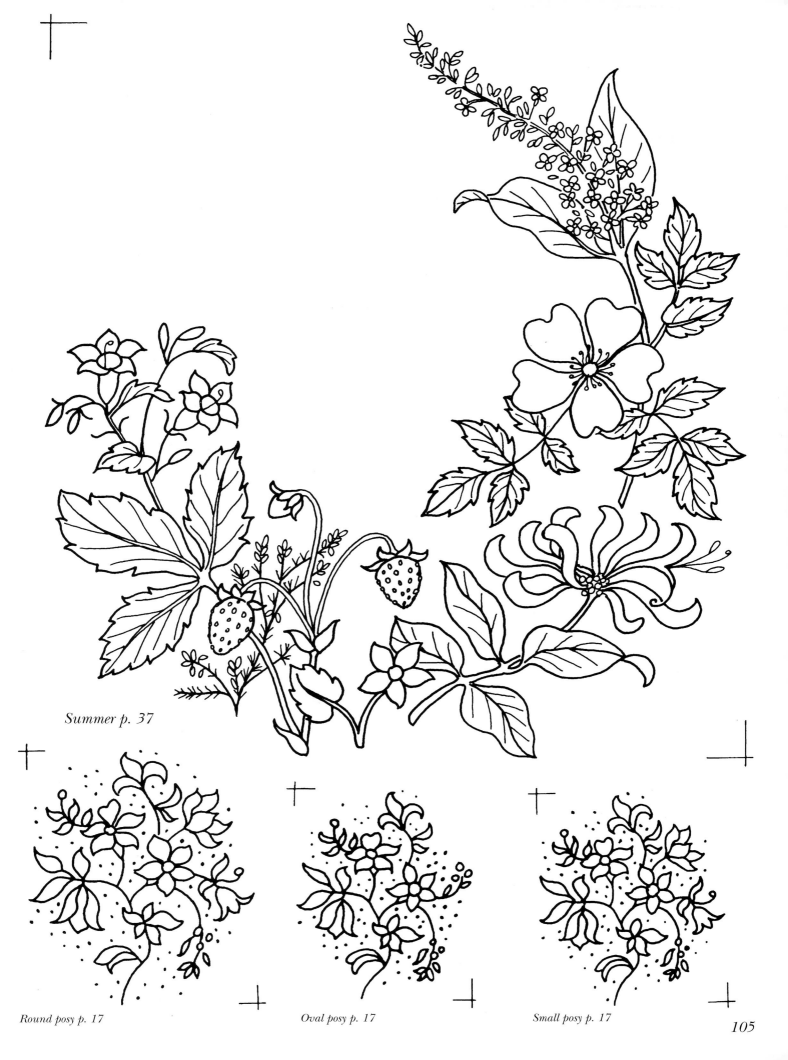

Summer p. 37

Round posy p. 17

Oval posy p. 17

Small posy p. 17

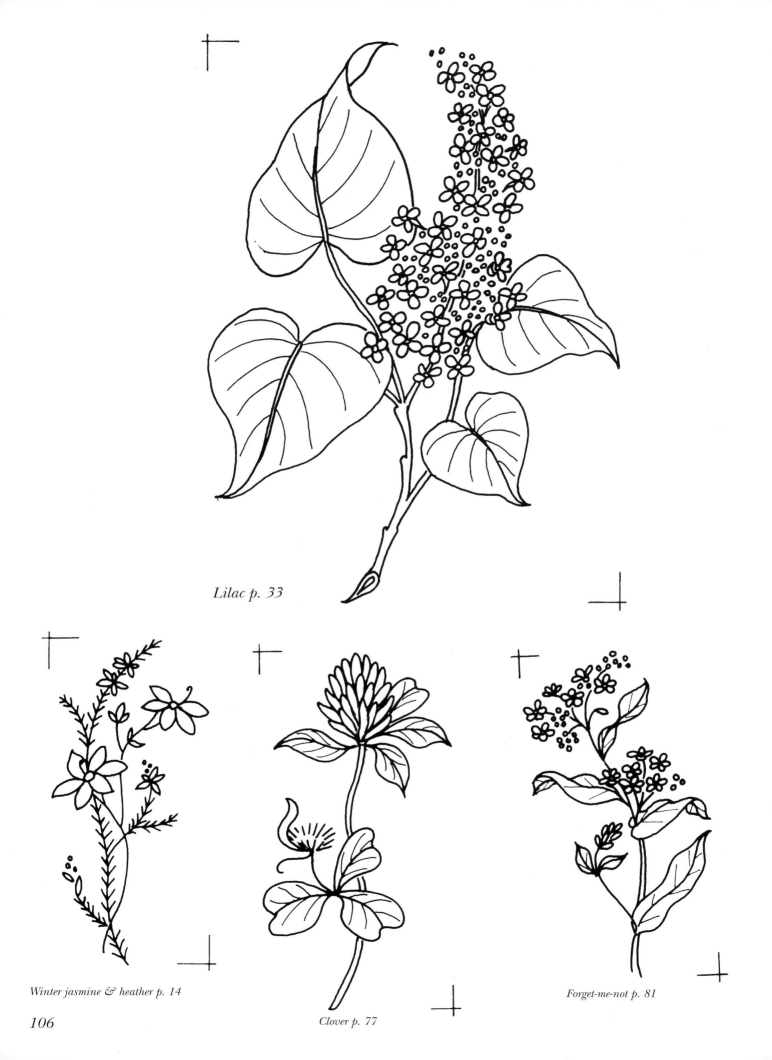

Lilac p. 33

Winter jasmine & heather p. 14

Clover p. 77

Forget-me-not p. 81

Apples p. 97

All leaves in long & short stitch

Underside in satin stitch

Long & short stitch interspersed with adjacent rows of split stitch

Long & short stitch

French knot at each centre

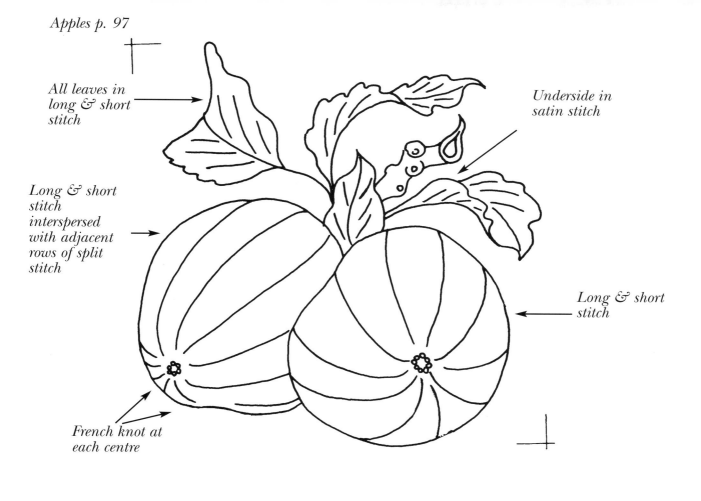

Four seasons, frontispiece

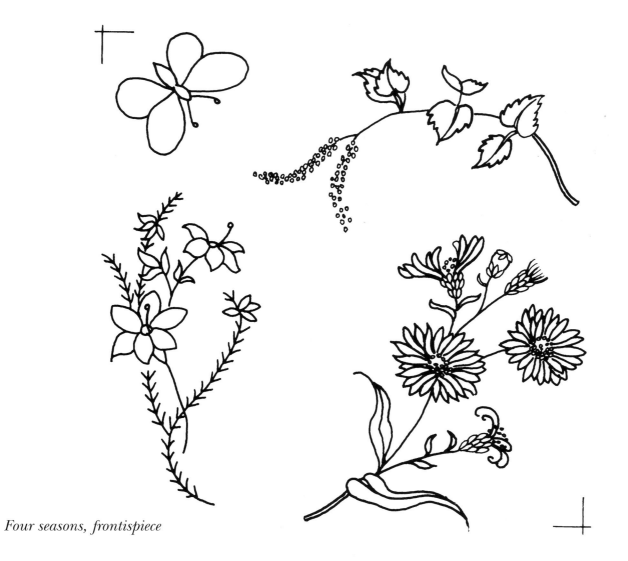

Daffodils & pussy willow p. 93

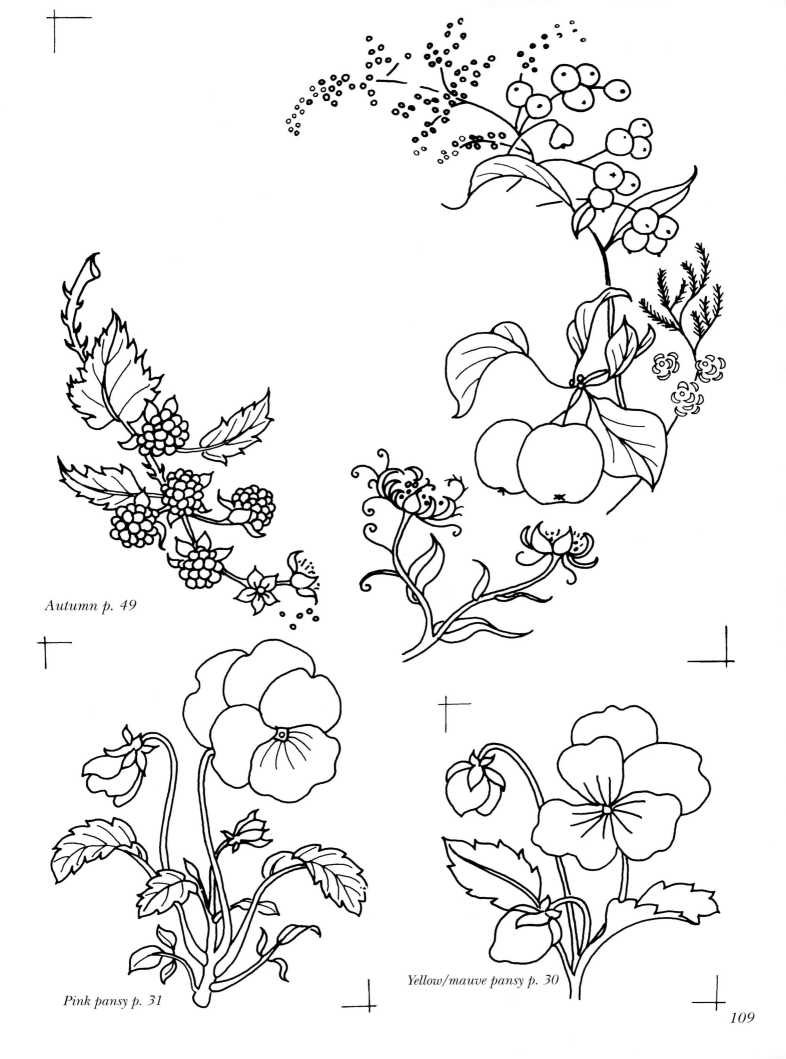

Autumn p. 49

Pink pansy p. 31

Yellow/mauve pansy p. 30

109

2.11

15

15

11

1, 2, 12

5

4

15

3

1

2,
11

7

14

6

1

2, 4, 11

15

10

13

1

8

7

2

9

2

6

10

9

Poppies p. 91

Suppliers

Most materials should be available from your normal supplier. Many suppliers hold thread conversion tables and can provide close equivalents from their own range if necessary.

Several mail order suppliers are listed below and others can be found in needlecraft magazines, or with the help of local groups.

Padding

Vilene padding is widely used in this book for raised petals and leaves and is readily obtainable in the UK. Use Vilene 240 white, extra heavy sew-in, which is about 1/16 in (1.6 mm) thick and 200 gsm in density. In the USA and Canada Pellon 70W is an alternative, though a little thicker than Vilene 240.

United Kingdom

Some shops supplying by mail order

Barnyarns, Canal Wharf, Bondgate Green, Ripon, N. Yorks HG4 1AQ, www.barnyarns.com

Mace and Nairn, PO Box 5626, Northampton NN7 2BF, www.maceandnairn.com

Stitches Needlecraft Centre, 355 Warwick Rd, Solihull, W. Midlands B91 1BQ, www.needlecraft.com

Voirrey Embroidery Centre, Brimstage Hall, Wirrall CH63 6JA, www.voirrey.com

Willow Fabrics, 95 Town Lane, Mobberley, Knutsford, Cheshire WA16 7HH, www.willowfabrics.com

Dyes and advice on dyeing your fabric, as used for the cover embroidery, can be obtained from Kemtex Educational Supplies, Chorley Business & Technology Centre, Euxton Lane, Chorley, Lancs PR7 6TE, www.kemtex.co.uk

Frames and other display items are available from Framecraft, 3 Isis House, Lindon Rd, Brownhills, Walsall, W. Midlands WS8 7BW, www.framecraft.co.uk

Germany

Tentakulum, Liebfrauenstr 1-3, 60313 Frankfurt-am-Main, www.tentakulum.de

Australia

Bustle & Bows, 164 Union Rd, Surrey Hills, Victoria 3127, www.bustleandbows.com.au

Mosman Needlecraft, Shop 24, Mosman Cache, 710 Military Rd, Mosman, NSW 2088, mosmanneedlecraft@bigpond.com

Needleworld, 109 King William Rd, Hyde Park, SA 5061, www.needleworld.com.au

Stadia Handcrafts, Australian Heritage Village, Corner Antill St & Federal Highway, Watson, ACT 2602, www.stadia.com.au

New Zealand

The Embroiderer, 140 Hinemoa St, Birkenhead, Auckland 10, theembroiderer@hotmail.com

South Africa

Stitchery Cottage, 7 Ann Arbor Pl, Glendower, Edenvale 1609, stitcherycottage@tiscali.co.za

USA and Canada

Nordic Needle Inc, 1314 Gateway Dr SW, Fargo, ND 58103 USA, www.nordicneedle.com

Access Commodities, PO Box 1355, Terrell, TX 75160, access1129@hotmail.com

D & J Needlework, 435 Bowen Island Trunk Rd, Bowen Island, BC V0N 1G0 Canada, www.dandjneedlework.com

---

A new embroidery book by Carol Andrews
from Ruth Bean Publishers

Making Needlework Accessories Embroidered with Beads
Use silks, couched threads and sparkling beads to create stunning needlework accessories - from needle books, bodkin and pin holders to thimble slippers, scissors cases and key fobs. Beautifully illustrated in colour with detailed instructions and diagrams.
ISBN 0-903585-33-2 240x210mm, 128p, 40 col + 160 bw ills, sewn paperback.

'The straightforward instructions make for enjoyable and tempting stitching...'
New Stitches, No 143

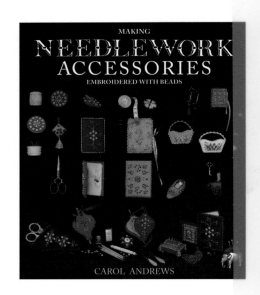